Growth of
Government
in the West

Growth of Government in theWest

G. Warren Nutter

American Enterprise Institute for Public Policy Research
Washington, D.C.

G. Warren Nutter is Paul Goodloe McIntire Professor of Economics at the University of Virginia and an adjunct scholar of the American Enterprise Institute.

Library of Congress Cataloging in Publication Data

Nutter, G. Warren.
    Growth of Government in the West.

    (AEI studies ; 185)
    1. Expenditures, Public.   2.   Government spending
policy.   3.   National income.   I.   Title.   II.   Series:
American Enterprise Institute for Public Policy
Research.   AEI studies ; 185.
HJ135.N84   336.3'9'091713   78–1674
ISBN 0–8447–3285–0

AEI studies 185

ISBN 0–8447–3285–0

Printed in the United States of America

CONTENTS

FIGURES

GROWTH OF GOVERNMENT
IN THE WEST

Government, it seems safe to say, is one thing that has been growing rapidly in the West. Wherever governments were once small they have become big, and wherever they were big they have become bigger. Nothing is so rare as a shrinking government.

When we speak of the size of government, we seem to have in mind the scope of activities within its purview, a concept not easily quantified. If we narrow the concept to government's command over a nation's resources, we can construct a partial measure of size by comparing government spending with the national product. Such a measure does not tell the whole story because it does not take account of such things as government lending or private spending that government mandates by law and regulation. Direct government spending as a fraction of national product is nonetheless a useful and widely used first approximation to the size of government.

There remains the problem of choosing the best measure of national product to use as the base of comparison. The most common practice is to compare government spending with gross national product, but that gross measure of output is inappropriate simply because it includes product that must be used to replace capital consumed in the course of production. Turning to measures of net production excluding capital consumption, we are finally faced with a choice between net national product evaluated at market prices and national income evaluated at factor cost. Which is the most appropriate base of comparison?

The answer is implied by the fact that government spends money predominantly to hire resources or to transfer income, an analogous transaction. In both cases government is exercising command over

I am indebted to William Nutter for valuable assistance in research, and to Marvin Kosters and Daniel Larkins for help on analytical problems.

1

resources at factor cost. Normally, only a relatively small part of government spending goes for the purchase of products at market prices. We are therefore led to conclude that size of government is most appropriately measured by government spending as a fraction of national income (evaluated at factor cost).[1]

In this study, we present first some evidence on what has happened in sixteen Western democracies over the last quarter century to expenditures at all levels of government as a fraction of national income. We then take a closer look at what has happened in the United States alone since 1929, almost half a century ago. Our purpose is to describe what has happened, not to analyze or explain why, a task we hope will be stimulated by the evidence presented here.

The democracies covered in the comparative study are ones for which reasonably complete and comparable data are available: Australia, Austria, Belgium, Canada, Denmark, France, the Federal Republic of Germany, Italy, Japan, Luxembourg, the Netherlands, Norway, Sweden, Switzerland, the United Kingdom, and the United States. Comparability in the national accounts of these countries is ensured to some degree by their association with the Organization for Economic Cooperation and Development (OECD), to which they report national accounts in accord with standardized concepts. We use these OECD data in comparing growth of government because they are the best available for that purpose, but they do involve some incomparabilities and discontinuities.[2] Care should be taken, therefore, in attaching significance to relatively small differences among measures for different countries or for different points of time in the case of a single country.

---

[1] This measure of the size of government does not lack problems of its own. For one thing, it overstates the command over use of resources exercised by government relative to the private sector of the economy, the overstatement varying directly with the extent to which domestic transfer payments enter into government spending. For example, there is no reason in principle why government spending could not reach 100 percent or more of national income, depending on the magnitude of domestic transfer payments and the taxation policy applied to them, even though ultimate use of resources would still be substantially determined by private spending. Government's relative command over a nation's resources would presumably be measured more accurately if transfer payments were included in some way along with national income in the base of comparison. But it is not clear to us how such an adjustment should be made. The question seems worthy of professional attention and discussion.

For those who are unconvinced by our line of argument and wish to compare government spending with the gross or net national product, we have provided figures on both for our sample of OECD countries in Appendix Table B-1.

[2] For further details on incomparabilities and discontinuities, see the appendixes to this study.

2

National accounts have been published by OECD for the period 1950–1974, but the series for some countries start later or end earlier. In the case of Australia, for example, the series covers only 1960– 1974. For Sweden, the set of accounts covering years before 1960 is incomplete and fundamentally incomparable with the set covering later years, so that useful data are limited to 1960–1974 in that case as well. For Luxembourg, reliable data do not extend beyond 1972. Finally, the longest period covered by all the series for the remaining thirteen countries is 1953–1973, and we shall therefore pay special attention to those years in the analysis that follows.

Little needs to be said about the data underlying the separate study of growth of government in the United States, since they are the familiar national income and product accounts of the Department of Commerce. We have been able to benefit from the major bench- mark revision of those accounts completed in January 1976.

Trends in OECD Countries

For our sample of OECD countries, the median percentage of national income accounted for by government expenditures was 34 in 1953, as shown in Table 1. That is to say, the percentages for half the coun- tries were at least as high as 34 or higher, while those for the other half were at least as low or lower.[3] If we confine our attention for the moment to the sample of thirteen countries for which we have requisite data for the entire period 1953–1973, we see that the median percentage rose steadily over the next two decades to reach 49 in 1973 (see the first column of Table 1). Essentially the same story is con- veyed by the median percentage for a sample of countries that varies over the years, covering the maximum number of countries for which data are available in each designated year (see the third column of Table 1). With the variable sample, the median percentage can be extended backward to 1950 and forward to 1974, falling to 31 in the former case and rising to 52 in the latter. From this evidence, it would seem that government expenditures for an average OECD country have risen from less than a third of national income in the early 1950s to more than half in the mid-1970s.

We might inquire next how the size and growth of government have been related to spending for external as opposed to domestic purposes. We see from Tables 2 and 3 that, on the average, external expenditures—the sum of defense spending and transfer payments to

---

[3] More precisely, the median percentage is the middle percentage in the sequence of percentages arrayed in ascending order for the countries covered.

3

Table 1
GOVERNMENT EXPENDITURES AS A PERCENTAGE OF NATIONAL INCOME: MEDIAN AND RANGE FOR SAMPLES OF OECD COUNTRIES, SELECTED YEARS, 1950–1974

| Year | Fixed Sample[a] | | Variable Sample[b] | |
	Median[c]	Range[d]	Median[c]	Range[d]
1950			31	22–39
1953	34	19–44	34	19–44
1955	35	19–42	35	19–42
1960	39	22–43	38	22–43
1965	41	25–49	42	25–48
1970	48	24–57	48	24–57
1973	49	27–62	49	27–62
1974			52	29–64

[a] Covers the same thirteen countries in all years, excluding Australia, Luxembourg, and Sweden.

[b] Covers varying countries: nine in 1950; fourteen in 1953 and 1955; sixteen in 1960, 1965, and 1970; fifteen in 1973; and thirteen in 1974. For lack of data, the following countries are excluded in the designated years: Australia, Belgium, Italy, Japan, Luxembourg, Norway, and Sweden in 1950; Australia and Sweden in 1953 and 1955; Luxembourg in 1973; and Austria, Italy, Luxembourg, and the United States in 1974.

[c] The middle percentage in the sequence of percentages arranged in ascending order for the countries covered.

[d] The lowest and highest percentages recorded for the countries covered.

Source: Derived from Appendix Table B-3.

foreigners—have represented a much smaller fraction of national income than domestic expenditures, and the disparity between the two has grown sharply over the period under review. The median percentage of national income accounted for by external expenditures drifted downward in the early 1950s, and wiggled down and up in succeeding years without an obvious trend. For the period as a whole, the trend seems to have been moderately downward, the median percentage falling from about 6 in 1950 to less than 5 in 1974. By contrast, the median percentage accounted for by domestic expenditures has risen steadily, from 28 in 1950 to 48 in 1974.[4] Trends in median percentages of national income accounted for by total, external, and

---

[4] Because of the way in which medians are calculated, there is no reason to expect those for components of an item to sum precisely to that for the item itself. For this reason, the medians in Tables 2 and 3 for a given year do not generally sum to the median in Table 1 for the same year; nor do the components in Tables 2 and 3 generally sum to totals.

Table 2

EXTERNAL GOVERNMENT EXPENDITURES, BY TYPE, AS A
PERCENTAGE OF NATIONAL INCOME: MEDIAN AND
RANGE FOR VARIABLE SAMPLE[a] OF OECD COUNTRIES,
SELECTED YEARS, 1950–1974

	Median[b]			Range[c]		
Year	Total external expenditures	Defense expenditures	External transfer payments	Total external expenditures	Defense expenditures	External transfer payments
1950	6.1	5.8	0.2	0.9–8.2	0.9–7.6	0.0–1.5
1953	5.9	5.7	0.2	0.7–17	0.7–16	0.0–2.1
1955	4.4	4.2	0.2	0.2–12	0.2–12	0.0–1.9
1960	4.6	4.1	0.2	1.5–11	1.3–11	0.1–2.8
1965	4.8	4.2	0.3	1.3–9.6	1.2–9.2	0.1–2.6
1970	4.5	3.8	0.5	1.1–10	1.0–9.6	0.1–1.2
1973	4.4	3.5	0.6	1.1–7.8	1.0–7.3	0.1–1.4
1974	4.9	3.7	0.7	1.0–6.7	1.0–6.3	0.1–1.4

[a] Covers varying countries: nine in 1950; fourteen in 1953 and 1955; sixteen in 1960 and 1965; fifteen in 1970; fourteen in 1973; and nine in 1974. For lack of data, the following countries are excluded in the designated years: Australia, Belgium, Italy, Japan, Luxembourg, Norway, and Sweden in 1950; Australia and Sweden in 1953 and 1955; Switzerland in 1970; Luxembourg and Switzerland in 1973; and Austria, Denmark, Italy, Luxembourg, Sweden, Switzerland, and the United States in 1974.
[b] The middle percentage in the sequence of percentages arranged in ascending order for the countries covered.
[c] The lowest and highest percentages recorded for the countries covered.
Source: Derived from Appendix Table B-3.

domestic government expenditures are displayed graphically in Figure 1.

As shown in Table 2, one component of external expenditures, transfer payments, rose on the average relative to national income, while the other component, defense expenditures, fell. In fact, the median percentage of national income accounted for by external transfer payments more than tripled over the period under review, rising from 0.2 to 0.7. In the case of domestic expenditures (shown in Table 3), transfer payments also outpaced other domestic expenditures on the average. The median percentage of national income accounted for by domestic transfer payments grew from 7.3 in 1950 to 19 in 1974, or by 160 percent, while the median percentage accounted for by other domestic expenditures grew from 17 to 27, or by 59 percent.

Table 3

DOMESTIC GOVERNMENT EXPENDITURES, BY TYPE, AS A PERCENTAGE OF NATIONAL INCOME: MEDIAN AND RANGE FOR VARIABLE SAMPLE[a] OF OECD COUNTRIES, SELECTED YEARS, 1950–1974

	Median[b]			Range[c]		
Year	Total domestic expenditures	Domestic transfer payments	Other domestic expenditures	Total domestic expenditures	Domestic transfer payments	Other domestic expenditures
1950	28	7.3	17	19–33	5.6–16	13–25
1953	29	8.5	16	16–37	3.4–17	13–26
1955	29	8.6	18	17–35	4.6–17	12–23
1960	34	11.0	20	19–38	4.6–17	14–26
1965	37	12.0	23	24–44	5.5–21	18–30
1970	43	16.0	27	23–52	5.4–23	18–34
1973	45	17.0	28	26–57	5.9–27	19–36
1974	48	19.0	27	28–58	7.0–29	20–36

a For the composition of the variable sample, see Table 2, note a.
b The middle percentage in the sequence of percentages arranged in ascending order for the countries covered.
c The lowest and highest percentages recorded for the countries covered.
Source: Derived from Appendix Table B-3.

Confining attention to the fixed sample of thirteen countries, we may note that the largest governments—size being measured by government expenditures as a percentage of national income—were to be found in the Federal Republic of Germany, France, and the United Kingdom in the 1950s but in Denmark, the Netherlands, and Norway in the 1970s. It is interesting that Denmark had the third smallest government in the 1950s, while Japan and Switzerland have consistently maintained the two smallest governments throughout the period under review. If we consider the full sample of countries, we find that Australia has had the third smallest government since 1960 while Sweden has had one of the two largest since 1970.

The size of government in individual countries is traced over time in Figure 2. There seems to be little doubt that the trend has been almost continuously upward for every country.[5] In the case of countries whose size of government can be measured from the 1950s on-

---

[5] For statistical evidence on the trend and continuity of growth, see section 2 of Appendix C.

Figure 1

GOVERNMENT EXPENDITURES, BY TYPE, AS A PERCENTAGE OF NATIONAL INCOME: MEDIANS FOR VARIABLE SAMPLE OF OECD COUNTRIES, SELECTED YEARS, 1950–1974

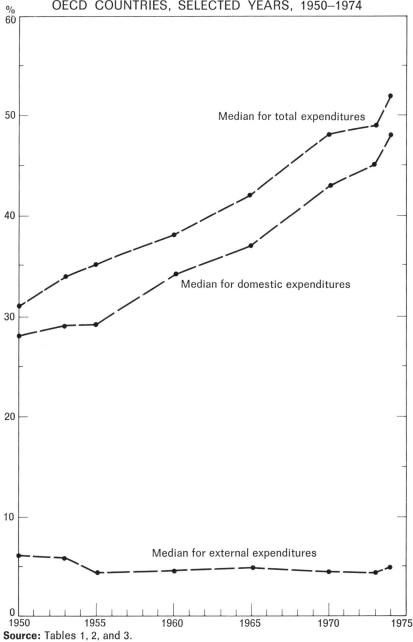

Source: Tables 1, 2, and 3.

Figure 2
GOVERNMENT EXPENDITURES, BY TYPE, AS A PERCENTAGE OF NATIONAL INCOME, OECD COUNTRIES, 1950–1974

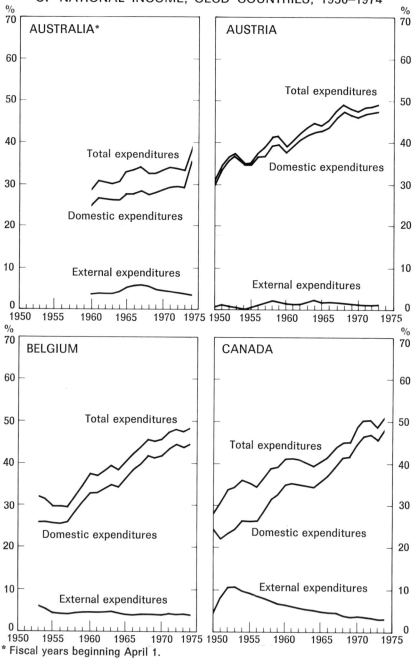

* Fiscal years beginning April 1.

Figure 2 (continued)

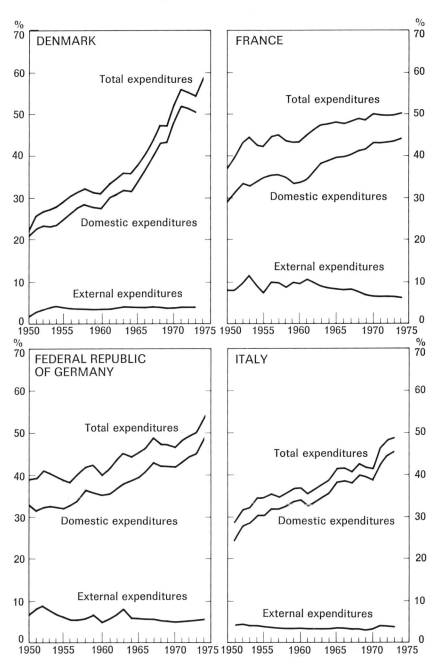

Figure 2 (continued)

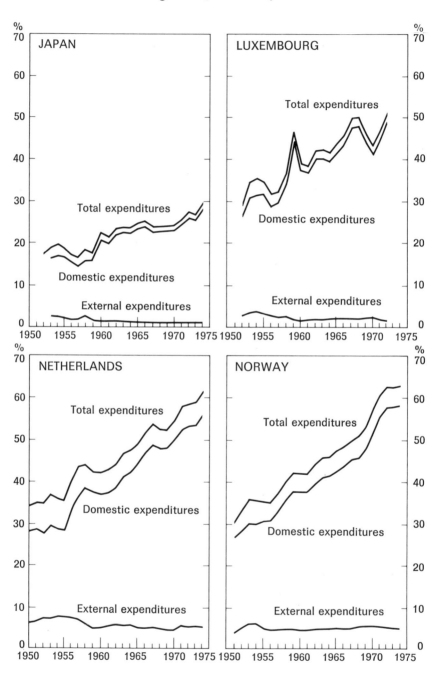

Figure 2 (continued)

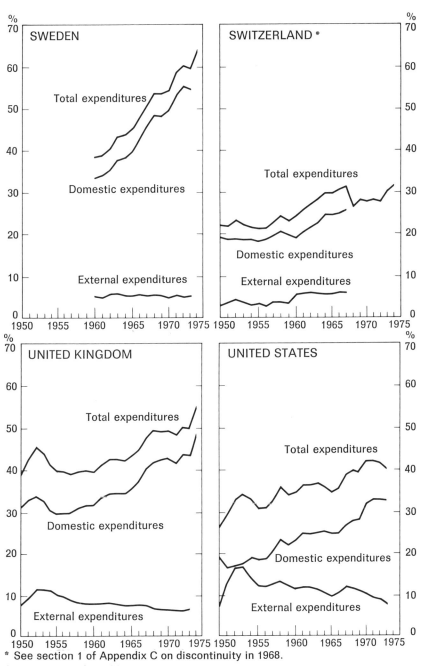

* See section 1 of Appendix C on discontinuity in 1968.

Source: Appendix Table B-3.

11

Table 4

ESTIMATED AVERAGE ANNUAL INCREASE IN GOVERNMENT
EXPENDITURES AS A PERCENTAGE OF NATIONAL INCOME:
SIXTEEN OECD COUNTRIES, VARYING PERIODS, 1950–1974

	Average Annual Increase (percentage points)	Period
Sweden	1.84	1960–1974
Denmark	1.42	1950–1974
Norway	1.38	1951–1974
Netherlands	1.13	1950–1974
Belgium	1.00	1953–1974
Luxembourg	.92	1952–1972
Canada	.82	1950–1974
Italy	.72	1951–1973
Austria	.66	1950–1973
Switzerland	.62[a]	1950–1969
United Kingdom	.55	1950–1974
Federal Republic of Germany	.54	1950–1974
United States	.51	1950–1973
Japan	.49	1952–1974
Australia	.46	1960–1974
France	.44	1950–1974

[a] Taken for the series based on former SNA (see Appendix A) because the
composite series is significantly biased. See section 1 of Appendix C.
Note: The estimated average annual increase is derived for each country from
a linear regression of government expenditures as a percentage of national
income on a time trend. In the case of countries with more than one OECD
series, the regression coefficient is taken from the composite series. See
Appendix Table C-3.
Source: Appendix Table C-3.

ward, there is an inverse relation between size of government in 1953
and growth of government over the period 1953–1973: the smaller
governments in 1953 have grown relatively more (in general) since
then than the larger ones. But the relation is not strong and may re-
flect peculiarities of the particular years involved.[6] If we smooth out
fluctuations in size of government by fitting a linear trend line to the
time series for each country, we can use the average annual increases
derived from those lines—the linear regression coefficients—as measures of growth of government (see Table 4). In these terms, Sweden,
Denmark, and Norway have had the three fastest growing govern-

---

[6] A rank correlation relating size and growth of government is given in section 3
of Appendix C.

ments, while France, Australia, and Japan have had the three slowest. But even in the latter cases the percentage of national income accounted for by government expenditures has been growing by almost half a percentage point a year, on the average.

It would be interesting to know whether governments have generally become more centralized as they have grown larger, but the OECD data available on this question are unfortunately too fragmentary and unreliable to provide a clear answer. Such evidence as there is indicates that the opposite has happened in the period under review, namely, that spending has grown somewhat faster at local levels of government than at the central level.[7] But, because of deficiencies in the underlying data, it is doubtful that much significance can be attached to this finding.[8]

Trends in the United States

Between 1929 and 1976, spending at all levels of government in the United States multiplied 3.5 times relative to national income, rising from 12 percent of national income in 1929 to 42 percent in 1976 (see Table 5 and Figure 3). In the same sense, external government expenditures multiplied 7.3 times relative to national income, and domestic government expenditures 3.2 times. Within domestic expenditures, however, transfer payments multiplied 12.3 times relative to national income, the most dramatic increase in these categories (see Table 6). Over the same period, federal government spending ran from 26 percent of total government spending to 68 percent (see Table 7). In all cases there have been fluctuations about the trend as government expanded differently in response to domestic and foreign affairs (see Tables 5 through 7 and Figures 3 and 4).

During the 1930s government was preoccupied with domestic affairs as the nation coped with the Great Depression. From 1929 through 1939 government spending doubled as a fraction of national income, rising from 12 percent to almost 25 percent. The increase had, in fact, taken place by 1932, but that growth occurred because national income fell by half, while government spending remained roughly constant, both being measured in current dollars. Under the New Deal, both then grew in current dollars at roughly the same percentage rate through 1939, by which time real national income

---

[7] See section 4 of Appendix C.
[8] For example, the OECD data for the United States on central government expenditures imply a much lower ratio of central government expenditures to total government expenditures than the standard Department of Commerce data, the difference in ratios increasing over time. See section 4 of Appendix C.

Figure 3
GOVERNMENT EXPENDITURES, BY TYPE, AS A PERCENTAGE OF NATIONAL INCOME:
UNITED STATES, 1929–1976

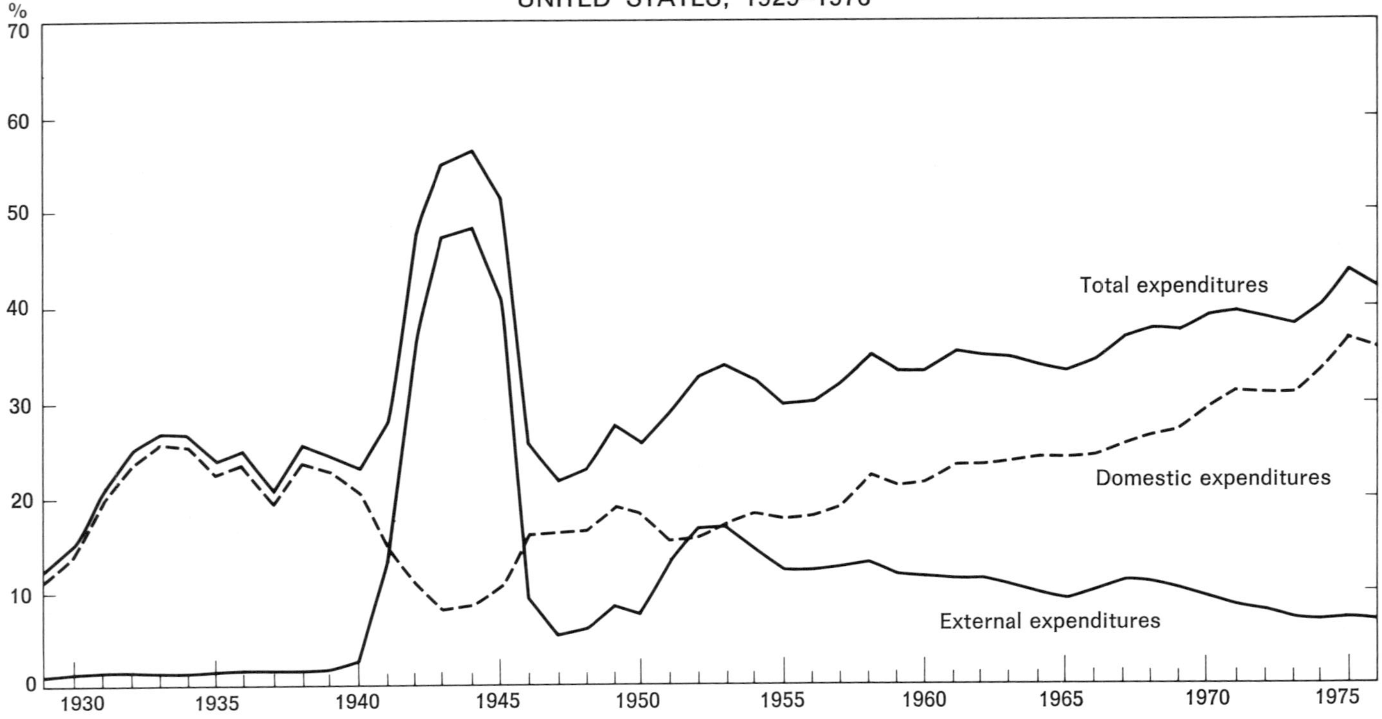

Source: Appendix Table B-4.

14

Table 5

GOVERNMENT EXPENDITURES, BY TYPE, AS A PERCENTAGE OF NATIONAL INCOME: UNITED STATES, SELECTED YEARS, 1929–1976

Year	Total Expenditures	External Expenditures	Domestic Expenditures
1929	12.1	0.9	11.2
1934	26.4	1.3	25.1
1939	24.6	1.8	22.9
1944	56.6	48.0	8.6
1949	27.9	8.6	19.3
1954	32.4	14.3	18.1
1959	33.0	12.0	21.0
1964	34.0	9.9	24.1
1969	37.2	10.2	27.0
1970	39.1	9.5	29.6
1971	39.7	8.5	31.2
1972	39.0	8.0	31.0
1973	38.0	7.2	30.9
1974	40.3	7.1	33.3
1975	43.7	7.2	36.6
1976	41.9	6.6	35.3

Source: Appendix Table B-4.

had recovered to its 1929 level. Both external and domestic spending doubled as a fraction of national income in this decade, but external spending still amounted to only 1.8 percent of national income in 1939.

During the next decade, external affairs dominated the scene as the size of government moved up and down in response to the demands of war, demobilization, and subsequent threats to national security. External spending rose to a peak of 48 percent of national income in 1944 while domestic spending fell to 8.6 percent. The former then fell to 5.6 percent in 1947 while the latter rose to 19 percent. Between 1939 and 1949, the fraction of national income attributable to total government spending rose by about 3 percentage points, but that rise consisted of an increase of almost 7 percentage points for external spending offset by a decline of almost 4 percentage points for domestic spending.

Over the 1950s, the ups and downs of external affairs once again set the trend. Until 1958, domestic spending by government represented a smaller fraction of national income than in 1949.

Trends changed markedly in the mid-1950s and the 1960s, as

Table 6

EXTERNAL AND DOMESTIC GOVERNMENT EXPENDITURES, BY TYPE, AS A PERCENTAGE OF NATIONAL INCOME: UNITED STATES, SELECTED YEARS, 1929–1976

Year	External Expenditures			Domestic Expenditures		
	Total	Defense	Transfers	Total	Transfers	Other
1929	0.9	0.8	0.0	11.2	1.1	10.2
1934	1.3	1.3	0.0	25.1	3.2	21.9
1939	1.8	1.7	0.0	22.9	3.5	19.3
1944	48.0	48.1	−0.1	8.6	1.7	6.9
1949	8.6	6.2	2.4	19.3	5.5	13.8
1954	14.3	13.7	0.6	18.1	5.0	13.0
1959	12.0	11.5	0.5	21.0	6.4	14.7
1964	9.9	9.4	0.4	24.1	6.7	17.4
1969	10.2	9.9	0.3	27.0	8.2	18.8
1970	9.5	9.2	0.3	29.6	9.5	20.1
1971	8.5	8.2	0.3	31.2	10.5	20.7
1972	8.0	7.7	0.3	31.0	10.4	20.5
1973	7.2	6.9	0.2	30.9	10.7	20.2
1974	7.1	6.8	0.3	33.3	11.9	21.4
1975	7.2	6.9	0.2	36.6	14.0	22.6
1976	6.6	6.3	0.2	35.3	13.5	21.8

Source: Appendix Table B-4.

Table 7

FEDERAL GOVERNMENT EXPENDITURES AS A PERCENTAGE OF TOTAL GOVERNMENT EXPENDITURES: UNITED STATES, SELECTED YEARS, 1929–1976

1929	25.6	1959	69.4
1934	49.7	1964	67.0
1939	50.9	1969	66.0
1944	92.7	1974	65.3
1949	69.7		
1954	71.9	1976	67.6

Source: Appendix Table B-6. See also section 4 of Appendix C for coverage of federal and total government expenditures.

16

Figure 4

FEDERAL GOVERNMENT EXPENDITURES AS A PERCENTAGE OF TOTAL GOVERNMENT EXPENDITURES: UNITED STATES, 1929–1976

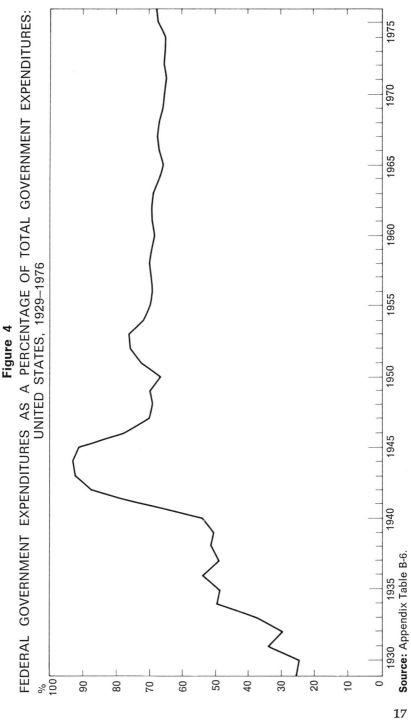

Source: Appendix Table B-6.

domestic considerations came once again to dominate growth of government. Despite the Vietnam War, the fraction of national income attributable to external spending remained relatively stable during this decade and a half, with minor fluctuations from year to year leading to a decline of 2 percentage points between 1955 and 1969. Meanwhile the fraction attributable to domestic spending rose rather steadily from 18 percent in 1955 to 27 percent in 1969. Government spending as a whole increased from 30 percent of national income in 1955 to 37 percent in 1969.

So far in the 1970s the fraction of national income attributable to domestic government spending has been drifting upward at an accelerated pace, rising by almost 10 percentage points in the six years between 1969 and 1975. This increase has been made possible by a decline of 3 percentage points for external spending and an increase of 7 percentage points for total spending. If domestic government spending is to continue rising at its present pace relative to national income, total government spending will have to accelerate relative to national income, because it will not be possible to reduce the share of external spending indefinitely.

As government grew through World War II, it became increasingiy centralized, but since then there has been a slight drift toward decentralization. Federal government expenditures rose from about a quarter of total government expenditures in 1929 to more than half on the eve of World War II, during which they rose to more than nine-tenths (see Table 7 and Figure 4). By 1947, the fraction had settled down at seven-tenths, and since then it has trended downward slowly,[9] reaching a level of around two-thirds in the mid-1970s.

Epilogue

Growth of government seems universal in the West. For the sixteen countries reviewed here, the percentage of national income accounted for by government expenditures has shown an average annual increase since World War II ranging from something less than half a percentage point in the case of France to almost two percentage points in the case of Sweden. Whether these trends will continue, accelerate, or retard is a mystery only the future can resolve. Meanwhile, let it be noted that, if government continues to grow in the United States at merely the established trend, within another decade or two it will rival its size at the peak for World War II, without the need of a war to make it so large.

---

[9] See section 4 of Appendix C.

Appendix A
SOURCE AND NATURE
OF BASIC DATA

1. Data for Sixteen OECD Countries

The basic source used to compile consistent and comparable statistical series on the growth of government in sixteen countries in the Organization for Economic Cooperation and Development (OECD) over the period 1950–1974 is the set of OECD yearbooks entitled *National Accounts of OECD Countries* and published before 1977. Since there is no single volume of historical OECD statistics covering the entire period, different segments of each series had to be taken from different yearbooks, and it is doubtful that an absolutely continuous series exists for any country because some revisions of data from one year to another introduce discontinuities of one sort or another that cannot be eliminated by use of published data alone. Furthermore, some essential data, such as defense expenditures for some countries and years, are not available in OECD publications and have, therefore, been taken from other sources.

For the OECD yearbooks published through 1971, the countries submitted data in accord with either the Standardised System of National Accounts[1] or the original UN System of National Accounts,[2] both of which we shall call the "former SNA." Beginning with the yearbook published in 1972, the countries were to reconstruct their data to conform to the new and fundamentally revised UN System of National Accounts,[3] which we shall call the "present SNA."

---

[1] *A Standardised System of National Accounts*, 1958 ed. (Paris: Organization for European Economic Co-operation, 1959).
[2] *A System of National Accounts and Supporting Tables*, Series F, No. 2, Rev. 2 (New York: United Nations, 1964).
[3] *A System of National Accounts*, Series F, No. 2, Rev. 3 (New York: United Nations, 1968).

The extent to which accounts have been reconstructed to conform with the concepts of the present SNA has varied from one country to another, so that there is little uniformity among countries in the periods of time covered by series based on former and present SNA. A synopsis of series by country is presented in Appendix Table A-1. Note that no series based on present SNA begins earlier than 1960. The beginning year for series based on former SNA is 1950 with the following exceptions: 1951 for Italy and Norway, 1952 for Japan and Luxembourg, and 1953 for Belgium. The series based on former SNA run at least through 1968 and extend to varied later years for all countries but Canada. The source of data for the different series is given in Appendix Table A-2.

While revisions in accounting concepts have varied in the described way, all data for 1969 onward have been reported in the terminology of the present SNA, regardless of the concepts underlying them. That is to say, all OECD series published since 1971 are presented in the format of the present SNA, whether the basic data conform conceptually to the former SNA or to the present SNA. Appendix Table A-3 sets forth the terminology in the former and present SNA that is equivalent in this formal sense, and identifies the items in those accounts that correspond to the summary accounts used in this study.

2. Data for the United States

The data used for the separate study of growth of government in the United States over 1929–1976 are drawn from the national income and product accounts of the Department of Commerce as published after the bench-mark revision completed in January 1976. Since those basic data are readily available in current and historical statistics,[4] we have not considered it necessary to recompile or reproduce them here. We do, however, give in Appendix Table B-4 the derived measures of government expenditures, by type, as a percentage of national income; and in Appendix Table B-6, federal government expenditures as a percentage of total government expenditures.

---

[4] For example, U.S. Department of Commerce, *The National Income and Product Accounts of the United States, 1929–74* (Washington, D.C., 1977).

Table A-1

PERIODS COVERED BY OECD NATIONAL ACCOUNTS, BY COUNTRY AND SYSTEM OF ACCOUNTS

	Former SNA	Present SNA
Australia		1960–1974
Austria		
Series 1	1952–1969	
Series 2	1960–1973[a]	
Belgium	1953–1974	
Canada	1950–1968	1960–1974
Denmark	1950–1971	1962–1974[a]
France		
Series 1	1950–1969	
Series 2	1960–1972	1970–1973[b]
Federal Republic of Germany		
Series 1	1950–1968	
Series 2	1960–1974	
Italy	1951–1973	
Japan	1952–1974	
Luxembourg	1952–1972	1962–1973
Netherlands	1950–1972	1962–1974
Norway	1951–1971	1967–1974
Sweden	1950–1969	1960–1974[a]
Switzerland		
Series 1	1950–1973[c]	
Series 2	1968–1974[d]	
United Kingdom	1950–1969	1960–1974
United States	1950–1972	1968–1973

[a] Data for 1974 are incomplete and, in some cases, preliminary. For Austria, we have not used the data for 1974 on the ground that they seemed to be preliminary estimates inconsistent with data for earlier years.
[b] For certain aggregates, series extends back to 1963.
[c] Data for 1970–1973 are incomplete.
[d] Data for all years are incomplete.

Table A-2

SOURCE OF OECD NATIONAL ACCOUNTS,
BY COUNTRY AND SYSTEM OF ACCOUNTS

	Years for Which Data Were Taken from OECD Yearbook Published in[a]					
	1970	1971	1973	1974	1975	1976
Australia[b]						
Present SNA			1960	1961	1962	1963–1974
Austria (series 1)[c]						
Former SNA	1950–1952	1953–1969				
Austria (series 2)[c]						
Former SNA			1960	1961	1962	1963–1973
Belgium						
Former SNA		1953–1959	1960	1961	1962	1963–1974
Canada						
Former SNA	1950–1952	1953–1968	1960	1961		
Present SNA[d]					1962	1963–1974
Denmark[e]						
Former SNA	1950–1952	1953–1959	1960	1961–1971		
Present SNA					1962	1963–1974
France (series 1)[c,d]						
Former SNA	1950–1952	1953–1969				

22

France (series 2) [c,d]						
Former SNA			1960	1961–1972		
Present SNA						1963–1973
Federal Republic of Germany (series 1) [f]						
Former SNA	1950–1952	1953–1968				
Federal Republic of Germany (series 2) [f]						
Former SNA			1960	1961	1962	1963–1974
Italy						
Former SNA	1951–1952	1953–1959	1960	1961	1962–1973	
Japan [e,g]						
Former SNA	1952	1953–1959	1960	1961	1962	1963–1974
Luxembourg [d]						
Former SNA	1952	1953–1959	1960	1961–1972		
Present SNA [h]					1962–1973	
Netherlands						
Former SNA	1950–1952	1953–1959	1960	1961–1972		
Present SNA					1962	1963–1974
Norway						
Former SNA	1951–1952	1953–1959	1960–1971			
Present SNA						1967–1974
Sweden [e]						
Former SNA [i]	1950–1952	1953–1969				
Present SNA [j]			1960	1961	1962	1963–1974

23

Table A-2 (continued)

	Years for Which Data Were Taken from OECD Yearbook Published in[a]					
	1970	1971	1973	1974	1975	1976
Switzerland (series 1) Former SNA	1950–1952	1953–1959	1960	1961	1962–1973	
Switzerland (series 2)[k] Former SNA						1968–1974
United Kingdom Former SNA	1950–1952	1953–1969				
Present SNA			1960	1961	1962	1963–1974
United States Former SNA[l]	1950–1952	1953–1959	1960	1961–1972	1968–1973	
Present SNA						

a The yearbooks are entitled *National Accounts of OECD Countries*. The one for (published in) 1970 covers 1950–1968; for 1971, 1953–1969; for 1973, 1960–1971; for 1974, 1961–1972; for 1975, 1962–1973; for 1976, 1963–1974.

b All data are for fiscal years beginning April 1.

c Because of unexplained revisions, the data published in 1973 and thereafter are inconsistent with those published in 1970 and 1971. We therefore treat the two sets of data as overlapping series, both in the former SNA.

d Defense expenditures from 1961 onward are taken from unpublished data provided by the United States Arms Control and Disarmament Agency (ACDA).

e Central government expenditures are published for fiscal years. These data have been converted into estimates for calendar years through linear interpolation.

f Series 1 excludes West Berlin and the Saar Valley, while series 2 includes them.

g Defense expenditures are derived from data for "national defense" for fiscal years beginning April 1 as given in the *Japan Statistical Yearbook* (Bureau of Statistics, Office of the Prime Minister, Tokyo). Data for 1950–1955 are from the 1966 yearbook, p. 489, table 314B; for 1956–1965, from the 1968 yearbook, p. 469, table 320; for 1966–1967, from the 1970 yearbook, p. 451, table 315A; for

1968–1974, from the 1973–74 yearbook, p. 447, table 314A. These data have been converted into estimates for calendar years through linear interpolation. There seems to have been an unexplained change in the coverage of defense expenditures in the 1970 yearbook, causing the series to be somewhat discontinuous between 1965 and 1966.

h Insufficient data are published to derive net national product and national income. For 1968–1972, these aggregates have been estimated as follows: net national product as gross national product (present SNA) minus the difference between gross national product (former SNA) and net national product (former SNA); national income as gross national product (present SNA) minus the difference between gross national product (former SNA) and national income (former SNA).

No data are published for external transfers of government. For 1968–1972, we have filled in the missing data by using external transfers from the series based on former SNA.

i Insufficient data are published to derive net national product and national income.

j Defense expenditures are not published for 1960–1962. We have filled in the missing data by using defense expenditures from the series in former SNA.

k Series 2, published in 1976, represents a major revision of series 1. See the note in the 1976 OECD yearbook, p. 287.

l In yearbooks published through 1971, interest on the public debt (property income payable by government) is published net of interest received by government (property income receivable by government). Beginning with the 1972 yearbook and applying to the years from 1960 onward, property income payable is published as a gross figure, property income receivable appearing as a current receipt of government. To make the series continuous, we have deducted property income receivable from property income payable from 1960 onward, so that property income payable is net of property income receivable in all years.

Table A-3

EQUIVALENT TERMINOLOGY OF FORMER SNA, PRESENT SNA, AND THIS STUDY

Summary Accounts Used in This Study	Equivalent OECD Terminology of					
	Former SNA			Present SNA		
	Table	Item	Nomenclature	Table	Item	Nomenclature
Gross national product (GNP)	1	8	Gross national product at market prices	1	8	Gross domestic product in purchasers' values
						plus
				1	10	Compensation of employees from the rest of the world, net
						plus
				1	11	Property and entrepreneurial income from the rest of the world, net
Net national product (NNP)	1	8	Gross national product at market prices	12	5	National income (including indirect taxes *less* subsidies)
			less			
	1	17	Depreciation and other operating provisions			
National income (NI)	1	18	National income	12	5	National income (including indirect taxes *less* subsidies)
						less

Category	Code	No.	Item	Code	No.	Item
Government expenditures				12	3	Indirect taxes *less* subsidies
	7 or 8	13	Total current expenditure [of government]	7 or 8	21	Current disbursements [of government]
			plus			*plus*
	7 or 8	19	Gross fixed asset formation [of government]	7 or 8	26	Gross capital formation [of government]
			plus			*plus*
	7 or 8	20	Increase in stocks [of government]	7 or 8	27	Purchases of land, net [by government]
						plus
				7 or 8	27	Purchases of intangible assets, n.e.c., net [by government]
Domestic expenditures of government			[Government expenditures][a]			[Government expenditures][a]
			less			*less*
	1	2a	Government current expenditure, defence	1	2b	Government final consumption expenditure, defence
			less			*less*
	7	12	Current transfers [of government] to the rest of the world	7	20c	Current transfers [of government], n.e.c., paid to the rest of the world
Domestic transfers of government	7	11	Current transfers [of government]	7	16	Social security benefits
						plus
				7	17	Social assistance grants
						plus

Table A-3 (continued)

Summary Accounts Used in This Study	Equivalent OECD Terminology of					
	Former SNA			Present SNA		
	Table	Item	Nomenclature	Table	Item	Nomenclature
				7	18	Current transfers [of government] to private non-profit institutions serving households
						plus
				7	19	Unfunded employee welfare benefits [from government]
						plus
				7	20	Current transfers [of government], n.e.c., paid to
						less
				7	20c	Current transfers [of government], n.e.c., paid to the rest of the world
Other domestic expenditures of government			[Domestic expenditures of government][a]			[Domestic expenditures of government][a]
			less			*less*
			[Domestic transfers of government][a]			[Domestic transfers of government][a]

28

		[Sum of items below]		[Sum of items below]
External expenditures of government				
Defense expenditures	1	2a Government current expenditure, defence	1	2b Government final consumption expenditure, defence
External transfers of government	7	12 Current transfers [of government] to the rest of the world	7	20c Current transfers [of government], n.e.c., paid to the rest of the world

a Derived as shown for this item where it appears in the left-hand column. Nomenclature applies only to summary accounts used in this study.

Appendix B
BASIC DATA

To derive growth statistics for the sixteen OECD countries, we considered it desirable to work with a single series of national accounts for each country spanning as many years as possible within the period 1950–1974. It was therefore necessary in the case of most countries to construct a composite series by linking together segments based on differing accounting concepts or methods. For example, the composite series for Canada consists of a segment based on former SNA covering 1950–1959 and a segment based on present SNA covering 1960–1974.

In the case of Belgium, Italy, and Japan, there was no need for a composite series since the national accounts published by OECD were not subjected to major revision and continued to be compiled on the same basis—former SNA—throughout the period 1950–1974. Similarly, the only series for Australia in the OECD accounts is one based on present SNA, beginning with 1960. For Sweden, we are also restricted to the series based on present SNA, beginning with 1960, because the accounts for earlier years based on former SNA do not contain sufficient data to permit calculation of national income. For special reasons noted below and in Appendix C, we decided not to construct composite series for Luxembourg but to use instead only the series based on former SNA and covering 1952–1972. For the remaining ten countries, composite series were constructed as described in the general note to Appendix Table B-1, which presents the national accounts used in this study.

In the case of each composite series, some discontinuity is bound to occur between the years at which different segments are joined together. From evidence reviewed in section 1 of Appendix C, we conclude that discontinuity introduces a significant bias into growth statistics only in the case of Switzerland. The bias would have been even more serious in the case of Luxembourg, and for this reason we decided not to construct a composite series for it.

Table B-2 gives the OECD accounts not used in this study because of the construction of composite series. These accounts underlie some of the analysis of composite series in Appendix C. Additional basic data are given in Tables B-3 through B-6.

Table B-1

NATIONAL PRODUCT AND GOVERNMENT EXPENDITURES: BASIC SERIES FOR OECD COUNTRIES, 1950–1974

AUSTRALIA
(million Australian dollars)

Year	Gross National Product	Net National Product	National Income	Government Expenditures						
				Total	External			Domestic		
					Total	Defense	Transfers	Total	Transfers	Other
1960	14,395	13,190	11,619	3,322	415	363	52	2,907	832	2,075
1961	14,721	13,442	11,896	3,646	463	398	65	3,183	915	2,268
1962	15,905	14,530	12,887	3,905	485	412	73	3,420	959	2,461
1963	17,666	16,133	14,361	4,308	531	444	87	3,777	1,060	2,717
1964	19,412	17,713	15,756	4,792	648	541	107	4,144	1,116	3,028
1965	20,332	18,479	16,342	5,388	848	721	127	4,540	1,190	3,350
1966	22,331	20,298	18,032	5,950	990	839	151	4,960	1,286	3,674
1967	23,797	21,575	19,098	6,505	1,128	976	152	5,377	1,346	4,031
1968	26,769	24,337	21,601	7,100	1,176	1,017	159	5,924	1,468	4,456
1969	29,554	26,912	23,893	7,791	1,162	983	179	6,629	1,667	4,962
1970	32,535	29,717	26,419	8,778	1,251	1,066	185	7,527	1,854	5,673
1971	36,342	33,260	29,569	9,999	1,306	1,100	206	8,693	2,168	6,525
1972	41,422	38,130	33,901	11,437	1,408	1,156	252	10,029	2,694	7,335
1973	50,358	46,770	41,420	13,761	1,611	1,322	289	12,150	3,321	8,829
1974	58,546	54,555	47,884	18,638	1,775	1,425	350	16,863	4,619	12,244

Table B-1 (continued)

AUSTRIA
(billion schillings)

Year	Gross National Product	Net National Product	National Income	Government Expenditures							
				Total	External			Total	Domestic		
					Total	Defense	Transfers		Transfers	Other	
1950	52.31	47.20	42.46	13.10	.39	.38	.01	12.71	4.10	8.61	
1951	69.61	63.13	56.89	19.66	.63	.62	.01	19.03	5.97	13.06	
1952	80.65	72.62	64.33	23.43	.48	.48	—	22.95	8.01	14.94	
1953	82.97	73.82	64.42	24.20	.44	.44	—	23.76	8.63	15.13	
1954	93.24	83.64	72.96	25.70	.03	—	.03	25.67	9.22	16.45	
1955	107.62	97.33	84.29	29.65	.20	.19	.01	29.45	10.11	19.34	
1956	118.01	106.53	92.46	34.82	1.07	1.06	.01	33.75	11.61	22.14	
1957	130.82	118.22	102.35	39.47	1.83	1.71	.12	37.64	13.15	24.49	
1958	136.67	123.26	106.76	43.91	2.16	1.99	.17	41.75	14.34	27.41	
1959	143.32	128.95	110.76	46.06	2.06	1.99	.07	44.00	15.35	28.65	
1960	163.25	146.18	125.61	49.49	2.02	1.89	.13	47.47	16.95	30.52	
1961	180.76	162.02	138.76	55.85	2.00	1.89	.11	53.85	19.53	34.32	
1962	192.35	171.97	147.55	62.30	2.15	2.07	.08	60.15	22.67	37.48	
1963	207.32	184.76	158.57	69.35	3.13	2.60	.53	66.22	25.10	41.12	
1964	227.14	202.79	173.09	77.43	3.96	3.41	.55	73.47	27.61	45.86	
1965	247.43	220.35	187.71	83.52	3.50	2.95	.55	80.02	30.10	49.92	

BELGIUM

(billion francs)

Year										
1966	267.57	238.37	201.75	91.75	3.92	3.47	.45	87.83	33.38	54.45
1967	283.16	252.04	213.74	102.53	4.13	3.62	.51	98.40	37.23	61.17
1968	302.76	270.17	226.90	111.45	4.17	3.72	.45	107.28	40.77	66.51
1969	331.73	296.50	248.86	120.45	4.43	3.96	.47	116.02	44.47	71.55
1970	371.24	332.41	278.64	132.78	4.62	4.09	.53	128.16	48.14	80.02
1971	412.70	369.45	308.71	149.62	4.77	4.14	.63	144.85	54.76	90.09
1972	469.41	420.20	349.27	170.53	5.47	4.74	.73	165.06	61.74	103.32
1973	533.27	476.73	396.58	195.12	6.09	5.14	.95	189.03	68.66	120.37

Year										
1953	411.3	373.0	335.7	106.7	19.4	19.1	.3	87.3	41.4	45.9
1954	428.4	387.8	351.1	109.8	18.3	17.8	.5	91.5	41.3	50.2
1955	456.5	413.6	371.5	110.8	15.7	15.2	.5	95.1	42.8	52.3
1956	487.3	440.1	395.8	118.5	16.9	16.4	.5	101.6	44.7	56.9
1957	516.7	466.4	418.7	124.5	16.6	16.1	.5	107.9	47.1	60.8
1958	520.7	470.1	421.8	136.8	17.7	17.3	.4	119.1	53.8	65.3
1959	536.6	483.3	430.1	148.3	18.2	17.6	.6	130.1	59.5	70.6
1960	571.5	515.2	457.5	170.9	19.3	18.8	.5	151.6	64.0	87.6
1961	606.4	547.8	481.3	178.6	19.3	17.8	1.5	159.3	66.0	93.3
1962	648.1	586.1	514.5	196.2	21.8	19.9	1.9	174.4	72.8	101.6
1963	696.0	628.8	551.0	217.5	24.6	22.5	2.1	192.9	79.1	113.8
1964	778.3	704.0	617.7	238.4	25.5	23.6	1.9	212.9	84.2	128.7
1965	848.9	768.9	676.7	271.8	26.6	24.7	1.9	245.2	104.6	140.6
1966	911.9	825.8	718.7	302.7	26.6	24.6	2.0	276.1	115.5	160.6
1967	977.3	884.9	767.0	334.6	30.2	27.0	3.2	304.4	126.1	178.3
1968	1,045.9	946.9	824.0	376.8	32.2	28.3	3.9	344.6	145.6	199.0
1969	1,159.7	1,050.8	916.5	416.0	36.1	31.4	4.7	379.9	157.7	222.2
1970	1,291.8	1,167.2	1,019.0	467.5	39.6	32.1	7.5	427.9	180.3	247.6

Table B-1 (continued)

Year	Gross National Product	Net National Product	National Income	Government Expenditures						
				Total	External			Total	Domestic	
					Total	Defense	Transfers		Transfers	Other
BELGIUM (billion francs)—continued										
1971	1,415.0	1,276.9	1,117.2	530.9	45.6	36.3	9.3	485.3	199.6	285.7
1972	1,579.2	1,429.6	1,264.4	607.9	48.4	40.6	7.8	559.5	233.3	326.2
1973	1,796.3	1,634.8	1,453.9	695.0	57.6	44.9	12.7	637.4	275.0	362.4
1974	2,105.6	1,920.1	1,705.9	823.6	62.2	49.9	12.3	761.4	333.4	428.0
CANADA (million Canadian dollars)										
1950	17,981	16,089	14,128	4,001	586	581	5	3,415	1,030	2,385
1951	21,147	18,967	16,555	5,000	1,340	1,331	9	3,660	1,032	2,628
1952	23,974	21,576	18,623	6,246	1,937	1,921	16	4,309	1,359	2,950
1953	25,003	22,357	19,267	6,637	2,033	2,008	25	4,604	1,461	3,143
1954	24,852	21,975	19,002	6,854	1,857	1,846	11	4,997	1,634	3,363
1955	27,108	23,862	20,690	7,275	1,894	1,870	24	5,381	1,737	3,644
1956	30,571	26,950	23,118	7,991	1,937	1,907	30	6,054	1,766	4,288
1957	31,885	27,898	23,950	8,669	1,884	1,844	40	6,785	2,076	4,709
1958	32,906	29,030	24,986	9,710	1,798	1,745	53	7,912	2,637	5,275
1959	34,909	30,730	26,433	10,344	1,704	1,632	72	8,640	2,755	5,885
1960	36,281	31,884	27,380	11,261	1,724	1,663	61	9,537	3,120	6,417

Year										
1961	39,393	34,368	29,530	12,157	1,792	1,715	77	10,365	2,709	7,656
1962	42,662	37,551	32,105	13,133	1,869	1,810	59	11,264	2,912	8,352
1963	45,695	40,131	34,417	13,827	1,801	1,712	89	12,026	2,979	9,047
1964	49,976	43,817	37,376	14,788	1,908	1,813	95	12,880	3,175	9,705
1965	55,020	48,159	40,875	16,431	1,778	1,659	119	14,653	3,423	11,230
1966	61,449	53,945	45,915	19,004	1,961	1,766	195	17,043	3,750	13,293
1967	65,989	58,170	49,318	21,709	2,182	1,965	217	19,527	4,667	14,860
1968	72,074	63,756	54,094	24,340	2,097	1,927	170	22,243	5,473	16,770
1969	79,251	70,675	59,953	27,080	2,084	1,899	185	24,996	6,161	18,835
1970	85,068	74,917	63,618	30,982	2,305	2,061	244	28,677	6,985	21,692
1971	92,816	82,110	69,834	34,943	2,380	2,132	248	32,563	8,255	24,308
1972	103,194	92,250	78,437	39,458	2,515	2,238	277	36,943	9,920	27,023
1973	119,575	106,637	91,238	44,219	2,716	2,405	311	41,503	11,200	30,303
1974	139,847	124,711	106,748	54,726	3,260	2,860	400	51,466	13,715	37,751
1950	21,481	20,297	18,383	4,200	362	333	29	3,838	1,247	2,590
1951	23,068	21,569	19,463	4,993	564	540	24	4,429	1,486	2,940
1952	24,604	22,898	20,695	5,549	702	674	28	4,847	1,622	3,220
1953	26,378	24,584	22,035	5,951	855	826	29	5,096	1,692	3,400
1954	27,628	25,705	22,880	6,334	971	936	35	5,363	1,704	3,650
1955	28,847	26,723	23,553	6,799	942	898	44	5,857	1,940	3,910
1956	30,880	28,537	25,105	7,664	982	916	66	6,682	2,093	4,580
1957	32,824	30,276	26,650	8,358	971	899	72	7,387	2,482	4,900
1958	34,331	31,640	27,706	8,908	1,016	927	89	7,892	2,645	5,240
1959	38,108	35,229	30,715	9,590	1,052	955	97	8,538	2,826	5,710
1960	41,131	37,986	33,092	10,301	1,168	1,045	123	9,133	3,009	6,120

Table B-1 (continued)

Year	Gross National Product	Net National Product	National Income	Total	Government Expenditures				Domestic	
					External			Total	Transfers	Other
					Total	Defense	Transfers			
DENMARK (million kroner)—continued										
1961	45,581	42,027	36,926	12,460	1,341	1,196	145	11,119	3,412	7,700
1962	50,978	47,016	40,991	14,245	1,672	1,509	163	12,573	3,933	8,640
1963	54,224	49,778	42,871	15,470	1,768	1,577	191	13,702	4,396	9,300
1964	61,984	57,079	49,185	17,582	2,029	1,790	239	15,553	4,762	10,790
1965	69,611	64,046	54,963	20,815	2,202	1,882	320	18,613	5,802	12,810
1966	76,381	70,174	59,624	24,180	2,349	1,974	375	21,831	6,874	14,950
1967	83,651	76,872	65,107	28,616	2,764	2,342	422	25,852	8,308	17,540
1968	92,188	84,678	70,879	33,445	2,896	2,372	524	30,549	9,970	20,570
1969	105,303	97,032	80,922	38,191	3,078	2,466	612	35,113	11,371	23,740
1970	116,467	107,144	88,960	46,748	3,424	2,716	708	43,324	13,539	29,780
1971	127,313	117,017	96,988	54,292	3,918	3,028	890	50,374	15,600	34,770
1972	143,982	132,134	109,243	60,664	4,251	3,196	1,055	56,413	17,925	38,480
1973	164,562	150,683	123,323	67,041	4,874	3,409	1,465	62,167	20,435	41,730
1974	183,714	166,257	138,972	81,632	...	...	1,830	...	24,300	...
FRANCE (billion francs)										
1950	100.23	90.75	76.47	28.50	6.27	5.80	.47	22.23	11.31	10.92

38

Year										
1951	122.95	110.60	91.98	36.08	7.41	6.90	.51	28.67	14.39	14.28
1952	144.04	129.34	106.90	46.27	10.66	9.81	.85	35.61	17.07	18.54
1953	150.39	135.59	111.82	49.65	12.77	11.86	.91	36.88	18.70	18.18
1954	159.19	144.18	119.31	50.88	10.54	9.60	.94	40.34	20.22	20.12
1955	170.50	155.20	129.58	54.90	9.57	8.36	1.21	45.33	22.42	22.91
1956	188.32	171.65	143.81	64.56	13.59	11.91	1.68	50.97	25.00	25.97
1957	211.11	192.59	160.84	72.49	15.32	13.53	1.79	57.17	28.43	28.74
1958	242.49	221.87	185.11	80.70	15.82	13.66	2.16	64.88	32.10	32.78
1959	272.62	248.78	208.13	90.29	20.38	15.97	4.41	69.91	35.35	34.56
1960	301.58	271.09	227.06	98.09	21.37	16.40	4.97	76.72	38.96	37.76
1961	328.33	294.98	247.45	110.54	25.85	20.40	5.45	84.69	44.50	40.19
1962	367.17	330.40	277.36	128.36	27.54	22.18	5.36	100.82	53.44	47.38
1963	411.99	370.65	310.39	146.72	27.71	22.85	4.86	119.01	63.51	55.50
1964	456.66	411.01	342.63	162.68	29.52	24.28	5.24	133.16	71.49	61.67
1965	489.83	439.80	367.76	176.84	30.62	25.30	5.32	146.22	78.80	67.42
1966	532.52	477.94	399.75	191.26	32.16	26.73	5.43	159.10	86.34	72.76
1967	574.77	515.00	433.34	210.10	34.90	28.91	5.99	175.20	94.59	80.61
1968	630.01	565.11	482.76	236.66	36.47	30.26	6.21	200.19	105.21	94.98
1969	723.50	649.84	551.64	266.99	37.75	30.70	7.05	229.24	120.91	108.33
1970	783.12	698.40	588.42	294.44	39.79	32.67	7.12	254.65	135.20	119.45
1971	871.34	778.41	654.60	325.37	43.44	34.91	8.53	281.93	152.52	129.41
1972	976.99	873.46	736.23	365.25	47.86	37.99	9.87	317.39	174.49	142.90
1973	1,108.15	991.22	835.32	415.46	53.89	42.28	11.61	361.57	201.93	159.54
1974	1,280.95	1,133.00	968.72	486.96	59.45	47.55	11.90	427.51	234.15	193.36

FEDERAL REPUBLIC OF GERMANY

(billion DM)

Year										
1950	97.9	87.82	75.16	29.52	4.97	4.38	.59	24.55	12.04	12.51
1951	119.5	107.53	91.08	35.88	7.29	6.16	1.13	28.59	13.40	15.19

Table B-1 (continued)

Year	Gross National Product	Net National Product	National Income	Government Expenditures						
				Total	External			Domestic		
					Total	Defense	Transfers	Total	Transfers	Other

FEDERAL REPUBLIC OF GERMANY (billion DM)—continued

Year	Gross National Product	Net National Product	National Income	Total	External Total	Defense	Transfers	Domestic Total	Transfers	Other
1952	136.6	123.30	103.77	42.58	9.07	7.52	1.55	33.51	15.75	17.76
1953	147.1	133.70	112.13	45.50	8.68	6.36	2.32	36.82	17.40	19.42
1954	157.9	144.26	121.08	48.02	8.45	5.96	2.49	39.57	18.35	21.22
1955	180.4	165.57	139.46	53.58	8.73	6.05	2.68	44.85	20.62	24.23
1956	198.8	182.27	154.37	59.20	8.46	5.48	2.98	50.74	23.01	27.73
1957	216.3	197.93	168.29	67.75	8.97	5.41	3.56	58.78	28.14	30.64
1958	231.5	211.31	180.14	75.72	9.98	6.04	3.94	65.74	31.69	34.05
1959	250.9	228.83	193.97	82.15	12.42	7.78	4.64	69.73	32.86	36.87
1960	302.3	276.57	235.73	94.92	11.70	9.64	2.06	83.22	37.61	45.61
1961	332.6	303.34	258.06	106.20	14.17	11.49	2.68	92.03	41.03	51.00
1962	360.1	326.62	277.49	120.66	17.90	15.06	2.84	102.76	45.05	57.71
1963	384.0	346.81	295.78	132.92	20.10	17.24	2.86	112.82	48.01	64.81
1964	420.9	379.73	324.27	144.45	18.71	15.87	2.84	125.74	52.86	72.88
1965	460.4	414.19	355.27	161.51	20.84	17.74	3.10	140.67	59.13	81.54
1966	490.7	440.02	377.12	174.31	20.36	17.78	2.58	153.95	64.42	89.53
1967	495.5	441.70	376.01	184.23	21.59	18.54	3.05	162.64	70.93	91.71
1968	540.0	482.60	416.89	197.03	21.66	16.78	4.88	175.37	74.37	101.00
1969	605.2	541.25	460.64	217.83	24.34	18.79	5.55	193.49	80.38	113.11
1970	685.6	610.82	529.19	246.46	25.03	19.84	5.19	221.43	86.90	134.53

1971	761.9	676.79	585.62	281.73	29.58	23.52	6.06	252.15	97.10	155.05
1972	833.9	740.35	639.14	315.52	32.88	24.59	8.29	282.64	110.21	172.43
1973	926.9	823.81	713.80	358.29	37.05	26.95	10.10	321.24	123.25	197.99
1974	994.0	878.25	763.73	413.37	40.61	30.28	10.33	372.76	141.95	230.81

ITALY

(billion lire)

1951	10,748	9,714	8,700	2,464	361	346	15	2,103	678	1,425
1952	11,591	10,475	9,318	2,954	394	380	14	2,560	894	1,666
1953	12,826	11.673	10,359	3,319	400	380	20	2,919	1,056	1,863
1954	13,656	12,455	10,939	3,796	438	427	11	3,358	1,231	2,127
1955	15,050	13,766	12,115	4,201	446	425	21	3,755	1,412	2,343
1956	16,394	15,010	13,144	4,656	468	461	7	4,188	1,630	2,558
1957	17,622	16,094	14,108	4,917	459	459	—	4,458	1,722	2,736
1958	18,923	17,314	15,233	5,430	495	491	4	4,935	2,009	2,926
1959	20,113	18,404	16,192	5,935	517	502	15	5,418	2,196	3,222
1960	21,828	19,971	17,507	6,462	565	548	17	5,897	2,330	3,567
1961	24,290	22,227	19,448	6,873	584	575	9	6,289	2,515	3,774
1962	27,303	25,017	21,958	7,994	677	656	21	7,317	2,962	4,355
1963	31,261	28,676	25,216	9,461	795	769	26	8,666	3,601	5,065
1964	34,179	31,275	27,591	10,576	831	811	20	9,745	3,913	5,832
1965	36,818	33,682	29,665	12,243	953	921	32	11,290	4,916	6,374
1966	39,829	36,460	32,235	13,332	1,010	978	32	12,322	5,376	6,946
1967	43,804	40,189	35,373	14,402	1,017	962	55	13,385	5,888	7,497
1968	47,280	43,431	38,393	16,318	1,151	1,058	93	15,167	6,709	8,458
1969	52,091	47,820	42,427	17,786	1,165	1,113	52	16,621	7,440	9,181
1970	58,261	53,270	47,219	19,527	1,428	1,175	253	18,099	8,199	9,900
1971	63,127	57,712	51,525	23,757	1,877	1,463	414	21,880	9,786	12,094
1972	68,880	62,927	56,817	27,280	2,075	1,619	456	25,205	11,225	13,980
1973	80,574	73,380	66,530	32,277	2,322	1,683	639	29,955	13,240	16,715

Table B-1 (continued)

JAPAN

(billion yen)

Year	Gross National Product	Net National Product	National Income	Government Expenditures Total	External Total	External Defense	External Transfers	Domestic Total	Domestic Transfers	Domestic Other
1952	6,263	5,829	5,275	906	...	...	—	...	158	...
1953	7,055	6,502	5,896	1,104	144	144	—	960	201	759
1954	7,831	7,130	6,465	1,261	156	155	1	1,105	302	803
1955	8,624	7,833	7,078	1,331	150	141	9	1,181	356	825
1956	9,726	8,792	7,977	1,384	145	135	10	1,239	359	880
1957	11,080	10,036	9,115	1,503	178	148	30	1,325	369	956
1958	11,522	10,393	9,410	1,725	243	151	92	1,482	444	1,038
1959	12,926	11,626	10,482	1,837	184	155	29	1,653	517	1,136
1960	15,498	13,908	12,596	2,818	190	161	29	2,628	585	2,043
1961	19,126	17,089	15,523	3,317	216	178	38	3,101	666	2,435
1962	21,199	18,786	17,109	4,003	239	208	31	3,764	796	2,968
1963	24,463	21,608	19,736	4,715	269	238	31	4,446	974	3,472
1964	28,932	25,419	23,336	5,497	303	272	31	5,194	1,163	4,031
1965	31,957	27,933	25,684	6,373	334	300	34	6,039	1,414	4,625
1966	36,822	32,061	29,565	7,432	384	336	48	7,048	1,637	5,411
1967	43,566	38,060	35,214	8,378	432	374	58	7,946	1,885	6,061
1968	51,593	44,923	41,644	9,921	478	420	58	9,003	2,180	7,263
1969	59,690	51,591	47,700	11,444	541	481	60	10,903	2,482	8,421
1970	70,731	61,245	56,699	13,633	631	567	64	13,007	3,042	9,965

LUXEMBOURG

(million francs)

Year										
1971	79,254	68,627	63,662	16,360	742	665	77	15,618	3,467	12,151
1972	90,611	78,235	72,535	19,739	879	778	101	18,860	4,291	14,569
1973	111,060	96,259	89,295	23,894	995	936	59	22,899	5,270	17,629
1974	132,473	115,239	107,841	31,553	1,130	1,064	66	30,423	7,490	22,933

Year										
1952	17,945	15,627	14,254	4,132	383	350	33	3,749	1,406	2,343
1953	16,563	14,187	12,821	4,390	441	407	34	3,949	1,526	2,423
1954	16,981	14,553	13,362	4,726	523	515	8	4,203	1,761	2,442
1955	18,448	15,878	14,665	5,111	473	466	7	4,638	1,976	2,662
1956	20,296	17,186	15,633	4,955	448	441	7	4,507	2,076	2,431
1957	21,935	18,516	16,867	5,457	402	393	9	5,055	2,349	2,706
1958	21,810	18,300	16,693	6,166	415	404	11	5,751	2,583	3,168
1959	22,482	18,750	17,308	8,045	310	294	16	7,735	2,753	4,982
1960	24,689	21,076	19,343	7,591	306	271	35	7,285	2,891	4,394
1961	25,340	21,827	19,988	7,732	322	290	32	7,410	3,014	4,396
1962	25,796	22,191	20,272	8,558	391	355	36	8,167	3,136	5,031
1963	27,496	23,696	21,678	9,194	392	348	44	8,802	3,368	5,434
1964	31,596	26,950	24,988	10,394	504	462	42	9,890	3,970	5,920
1965	33,117	27,917	25,648	11,201	527	477	50	10,674	4,542	6,132
1966	34,665	29,296	26,833	12,319	581	497	84	11,738	4,954	6,784
1967	35,412	29,568	27,037	13,469	553	413	140	12,916	5,655	7,261
1968	38,729	32,036	29,208	14,619	588	374	214	14,031	5,962	8,069
1969	44,515	36,752	33,296	15,363	773	391	382	14,590	6,510	8,080
1970	51,046	42,506	38,369	16,723	905	416	489	15,818	7,063	8,755
1971	53,868	45,648	40,406	18,932	824	442	382	18,108	8,209	9,899
1972	58,135	49,335	43,803	22,275	777	517	260	21,498	9,433	12,065

Table B-1 (continued)

NETHERLANDS
(million guilders)

Year	Gross National Product	Net National Product	National Income	Government Expenditures Total	External Total	External Defense	External Transfers	Total	Domestic Transfers	Domestic Other
1950	18,911	17,057	14,926	5,085	913	901	12	4,172	1,260	2,912
1951	21,650	19,461	16,917	5,857	1,073	1,060	13	4,784	1,470	3,314
1952	22,688	20,285	17,689	6,115	1,264	1,253	11	4,851	1,645	3,206
1953	24,200	21,800	19,110	6,985	1,342	1,330	12	5,643	1,776	3,867
1954	27,000	24,516	21,565	7,755	1,614	1,583	31	6,141	1,986	4,155
1955	30,276	27,528	24,525	8,680	1,794	1,699	95	6,886	2,152	4,734
1956	32,568	29,587	26,493	10,530	1,922	1,845	77	8,608	2,363	6,245
1957	35,364	32,040	29,044	12,530	1,962	1,882	80	10,568	3,158	7,410
1958	35,930	32,407	29,560	12,916	1,679	1,590	89	11,237	3,740	7,497
1959	38,443	34,735	31,444	13,150	1,481	1,397	84	11,669	3,889	7,780
1960	42,732	38,823	35,149	14,639	1,713	1,650	63	12,926	4,365	8,561
1961	45,288	41,082	37,045	15,718	1,944	1,813	131	13,774	4,724	9,050
1962	48,517	43,972	39,591	17,346	2,148	1,945	203	15,198	5,329	9,869
1963	52,858	47,918	43,130	19,983	2,265	2,287	−22	17,718	6,644	11,074
1964	62,154	56,695	51,079	24,102	2,700	2,573	127	21,402	7,863	13,539
1965	69,368	63,358	56,949	27,730	2,761	2,574	187	24,969	9,614	15,355

NORWAY

(million kroner)

Year										
1966	75,395	68,800	61,568	31,732	2,865	2,694	171	28,867	11,336	17,531
1967	82,997	75,831	67,759	36,248	3,329	3,044	285	32,919	13,080	19,839
1968	90,404	82,655	73,320	38,220	3,376	3,088	288	34,844	15,525	19,319
1969	102,365	93,797	84,113	43,782	3,550	3,286	264	40,232	18,288	21,944
1970	114,984	105,257	93,704	50,921	4,175	3,882	293	46,746	21,353	25,393
1971	129,850	118,510	104,720	60,370	5,690	4,460	1,230	54,680	25,840	28,840
1972	147,230	134,320	118,550	69,170	6,150	4,730	1,420	63,020	30,880	32,140
1973	166,480	152,150	135,100	79,060	7,000	5,140	1,860	72,060	36,090	35,970
1974	187,040	170,890	152,590	93,110	7,710	5,710	2,000	85,400	44,260	41,140
1951	18,684	16,586	14,950	4,513	560	544	16	3,953	903	3,050
1952	20,638	18,248	16,274	5,386	808	788	20	4,578	1,110	3,468
1953	20,874	18,408	16,524	5,912	988	958	30	4,924	1,239	3,685
1954	22,581	19,947	17,863	6,347	1,057	1,026	31	5,290	1,402	3,888
1955	23,995	21,139	18,914	6,667	884	866	18	5,783	1,542	4,241
1956	27,090	23,909	21,395	7,477	935	915	20	6,542	1,705	4,837
1957	28,788	25,201	22,567	8,423	1,007	985	22	7,416	2,001	5,415
1958	28,658	24,811	21,926	8,801	987	967	20	7,814	2,193	5,621
1959	30,417	26,239	23,087	9,710	1,052	1,031	21	8,658	2,595	6,063
1960	32,340	27,954	24,680	10,309	1,057	1,024	33	9,252	2,725	6,527
1961	35,239	30,569	26,897	11,189	1,142	1,104	38	10,047	2,982	7,065
1962	37,988	33,046	29,004	12,802	1,328	1,285	43	11,474	3,494	7,980
1963	40,970	35,738	31,571	14,415	1,443	1,375	68	12,972	3,925	9,047
1964	45,300	39,709	34,805	15,922	1,564	1,483	81	14,358	4,415	9,943
1965	50,211	43,893	38,649	18,283	1,906	1,815	91	16,377	4,916	11,461
1966	54,679	47,755	41,804	20,079	1,956	1,842	114	18,123	5,469	12,654
1967	60,132	52,520	45,927	22,914	2,120	2,013	107	20,794	6,374	14,420
1968	63,115	54,257	47,940	24,259	2,518	2,352	166	21,741	7,360	14,381
1969	68,881	59,309	51,819	27,557	2,772	2,550	222	24,785	8,474	16,311
1970	79,073	68,029	57,774	33,001	3,120	2,821	299	29,881	11,173	18,708

Table B-1 (continued)

Year	Gross National Product	Net National Product	National Income	Government Expenditures Total	External Total	External Defense	External Transfers	Domestic Total	Domestic Transfers	Other

N O R W A Y (million kroner)—continued

1971	88,318	75,912	64,170	38,901	3,308	3,035	273	35,593	13,606	21,987
1972	97,243	83,734	70,925	44,270	3,599	3,215	384	40,671	15,642	25,029
1973	110,100	94,942	80,856	50,368	3,947	3,497	450	46,421	18,201	28,220
1974	127,032	108,560	93,811	58,989	4,585	3,917	668	54,404	20,528	33,876

S W E D E N
(million kroner)

1960	72,107	65,458	58,999	22,692	3,020	2,974	46	19,672	6,139	13,533
1961	78,240	71,008	63,818	24,662	3,063	3,014	49	21,599	6,663	14,936
1962	85,285	76,770	68,029	27,696	3,709	3,626	83	23,987	7,332	16,655
1963	92,206	82,694	73,249	31,747	4,100	3,963	137	27,647	8,437	19,210
1964	102,872	92,501	82,093	35,609	4,405	4,260	145	31,204	9,425	21,779
1965	113,442	101,963	89,914	40,503	4,750	4,585	165	35,753	11,029	24,724
1966	123,389	110,744	97,097	46,563	5,385	5,137	248	41,178	12,428	28,750
1967	133,398	119,849	104,908	53,042	5,373	5,020	353	47,669	14,428	33,241
1968	141,598	127,307	110,859	59,252	5,871	5,456	415	53,381	16,239	37,142
1969	153,226	138,609	121,617	64,799	6,351	5,680	671	58,448	18,309	40,139
1970	170,783	154,670	135,286	73,341	6,476	5,862	614	66,865	20,476	46,389

SWITZERLAND
(million francs)

Year										
1971	50,887	24,316	75,203	679	6,824	7,503	82,706	141,509	165,862	183,482
1972	56,684	27,850	84,534	876	6,753	7,629	92,163	153,223	179,747	199,089
1973	60,924	31,049	91,973	938	7,651	8,589	100,562	168,742	198,328	220,180
1974	...	41,501	...	1,506	...	...	122,506	192,692	222,761	248,641
1950	2,335	970	3,305	20	480	500	3,805	17,250	18,420	19,920
1951	2,420	1,075	3,495	25	630	655	4,150	18,885	20,140	21,935
1952	2,555	1,175	3,730	10	835	845	4,575	19,785	21,065	23,020
1953	2,605	1,210	3,815	20	725	745	4,560	20,660	22,040	24,090
1954	2,725	1,360	4,085	20	635	655	4,740	21,985	23,455	25,555
1955	2,825	1,425	4,250	30	695	725	4,975	23,400	24,950	27,265
1956	3,015	1,625	4,640	35	625	660	5,300	24,965	26,745	29,285
1957	3,290	1,815	5,105	55	875	930	6,035	26,450	28,220	30,870
1958	3,625	1,965	5,590	55	940	995	6,585	27,175	28,930	31,520
1959	3,675	2,070	5,745	65	900	965	6,710	29,030	30,875	33,840
1960	4,465	1,450	5,915	875	850	1,725	7,640	31,285	33,515	37,055
1961	5,310	1,730	7,040	960	1,020	1,980	9,020	34,920	37,530	41,490
1962	6,290	1,975	8,265	1,100	1,180	2,280	10,545	38,780	41,655	46,050
1963	7,430	2,135	9,565	1,125	1,285	2,410	11,975	42,320	45,515	50,370
1964	8,500	2,855	11,355	1,150	1,400	2,550	13,905	46,570	50,090	55,540
1965	9,020	3,115	12,135	1,285	1,470	2,755	14,890	50,145	53,935	59,985
1966	9,935	3,425	13,360	1,620	1,615	3,235	16,595	54,015	58,025	64,625
1967	10,660	3,945	14,605	1,755	1,625	3,380	17,985	57,500	61,705	68,825
1968	...	7,125	...	200	...	...	17,185	64,485	68,870	77,170
1969	...	8,625	...	290	...	...	19,610	69,800	74,845	84,020
1970	...	9,325	...	300	...	...	21,350	77,545	83,160	93,930

47

Table B-1 (continued)

Year	Gross National Product	Net National Product	National Income	Government Expenditures Total	External Total	External Defense	External Transfers	Total	Domestic Transfers	Domestic Other
				SWITZERLAND (million francs)—continued						
1971	106,485	94,235	88,230	24,815	...	...	340	...	10,650	...
1972	120,535	106,445	99,430	27,725	...	...	410	...	11,585	...
1973	134,525	119,375	111,800	33,875	...	...	565	...	15,335	...
1974	146,295	130,165	122,755	38,755	...	...	640	...	17,400	...
				UNITED KINGDOM (million pounds sterling)						
1950	13,325	12,372	10,781	4,217	865	814	51	3,352	695	2,657
1951	14,749	13,648	11,845	5,044	1,139	1,074	65	3,905	720	3,185
1952	15,877	14,637	12,762	5,782	1,509	1,440	69	4,273	836	3,437
1953	17,052	15,763	13,760	6,044	1,590	1,521	69	4,454	926	3,528
1954	17,998	16,658	14,576	5,974	1,585	1,515	70	4,389	944	3,445
1955	19,281	17,820	15,515	6,139	1,535	1,465	70	4,604	1,035	3,569
1956	20,902	19,318	16,850	6,647	1,617	1,544	73	5,030	1,106	3,924
1957	22,121	20,430	17,871	6,936	1,596	1,521	75	5,340	1,169	4,171
1958	23,128	21,337	18,682	7,330	1,543	1,466	77	5,787	1,407	4,380
1959	24,293	22,449	19,618	7,778	1,594	1,512	82	6,184	1,555	4,629
1960	25,670	23,608	20,778	8,191	1,684	1,594	90	6,507	1,573	4,934

UNITED STATES

(million dollars)

Year										
1961	5,435	1,938	7,373	108	1,695	1,803	9,176	22,186	25,145	27,366
1962	5,818	2,141	7,959	110	1,817	1,927	9,886	23,255	26,436	28,790
1963	6,156	2,409	8,565	120	1,863	1,983	10,548	24,802	28,159	30,648
1964	6,700	2,548	9,248	151	1,943	2,094	11,342	26,913	30,724	33,391
1965	7,337	2,917	10,254	162	2,076	2,238	12,492	28,754	33,009	35,875
1966	8,084	3,188	11,272	163	2,164	2,327	13,599	30,365	35,065	38,168
1967	9,224	3,582	12,806	167	2,350	2,517	15,323	31,994	37,011	40,294
1968	10,179	4,109	14,288	156	2,374	2,530	16,818	34,171	39,851	43,434
1969	10,793	4,394	15,187	153	2,256	2,409	17,596	35,817	42,503	46,403
1970	11,949	4,839	16,788	151	2,420	2,571	19,359	39,275	46,540	50,974
1971	13,148	5,349	18,497	178	2,714	2,892	21,389	44,182	51,780	56,850
1972	15,033	6,525	21,558	178	3,017	3,195	24,753	49,432	57,252	63,043
1973	17,704	7,215	24,919	325	3,316	3,641	28,560	57,181	65,446	72,316
1974	22,997	8,771	31,768	275	4,133	4,408	36,176	65,472	73,587	81,928
1950	31,674	13,979	45,653	3,738	14,243	17,981	63,634	242,167	267,295	288,293
1951	34,724	11,215	45,939	3,267	33,555	36,822	82,761	279,232	308,147	332,957
1952	38,041	11,238	49,279	2,183	46,046	48,229	97,508	293,180	323,723	350,676
1953	42,156	12,066	54,222	2,084	48,715	50,799	105,021	306,635	340,328	369,720
1954	43,397	14,245	57,642	1,454	41,519	42,973	100,615	304,918	338,234	370,135
1955	45,526	15,343	60,869	1,522	39,607	41,129	101,998	332,175	368,028	403,711
1956	49,226	16,451	65,677	1,795	41,161	42,956	108,633	352,832	386,704	425,228
1957	54,553	19,297	73,850	1,740	44,577	46,317	120,167	368,187	405,538	447,859
1958	61,655	23,464	85,119	1,850	46,301	48,151	133,270	369,962	410,024	454,965
1959	63,858	24,264	88,122	1,882	46,809	48,691	136,813	402,355	444,068	491,236
1960	70,073	25,916	95,989	1,913	45,946	47,859	143,848	417,093	462,306	511,388

Table B-1 (continued)

| | | | | | Government Expenditures | | | | | |
| | | | | | External | | | Domestic | | |
Year	Gross National Product	Net National Product	National Income	Total	Total	Defense	Transfers	Total	Transfers	Other
				UNITED STATES	(million dollars)—continued					
1961	528,600	477,060	430,129	157,187	51,105	48,992	2,113	106,082	29,639	76,443
1962	569,122	512,726	460,613	168,112	55,130	52,950	2,180	112,982	30,360	82,622
1963	599,705	540,505	485,264	175,472	54,585	52,387	2,198	120,887	31,981	88,906
1964	642,837	579,215	521,739	184,979	54,040	51,862	2,178	130,939	33,053	97,886
1965	696,254	628,309	568,423	193,889	54,400	52,215	2,185	139,489	35,834	103,655
1966	762,722	689,416	625,128	218,792	65,486	63,205	2,281	153,306	39,518	113,788
1967	808,124	728,886	658,468	251,869	76,793	74,546	2,247	175,076	46,930	128,146
1968	867,437	782,035	706,210	277,468	82,993	75,939	7,054	194,475	54,069	140,406
1969	932,166	838,961	756,002	295,105	83,407	78,499	4,908	211,698	59,585	152,113
1970	987,862	878,650	788,158	330,644	80,175	75,392	4,783	250,469	72,305	178,164
1971	1,065,699	948,255	849,574	356,812	77,595	71,806	5,789	279,217	85,484	193,733
1972	1,168,371	1,040,862	936,503	388,760	81,969	74,917	7,052	306,791	94,809	211,982
1973	1,305,889	1,168,627	1,053,727	423,559	82,035	76,517	5,518	341,524	108,668	232,856

Note: The series given here are composed of the following components: *Australia:* 1953–1974, present SNA. *Austria:* 1950–1959, series 1, former SNA.; 1960–1973, series 2, former SNA. *Belgium:* 1950–1960, former SNA.; 1961–1974, present SNA. *Canada:* 1950–1959, series 1, former SNA.; 1960–1974, present SNA. *Denmark:* 1950–1961, former SNA.; 1962–1974, present SNA. *France:* 1950–1959, series 1, former SNA.; 1960–1969, series 2, former SNA.; 1970–1974, series 2, present SNA. *Federal Republic of Germany:* 1950–1959, series 1, former SNA.; 1960–1974, series 2, former SNA. *Italy:* 1951–1973, former SNA. *Japan:* 1952–1974, former SNA. *Luxembourg:* 1952–1972, former SNA. *Netherlands:* 1950–1967, former SNA.; 1968–1974, present SNA. *Norway:* 1951–1967, former SNA.; 1968–1974, present SNA. *Sweden:* 1960–1974, present SNA. *Switzerland:* 1950–1967, series 1, former SNA.; 1968–1974, series 2, former SNA. *United Kingdom:* 1950–1959, former SNA.; 1960–1974, present SNA. *United States:* 1950–1967, former SNA.; 1968–1973, present SNA. Ellipsis (...): not available. Dash (—): less than half a unit. **Source:** Table A-2.

50

Table B-2

NATIONAL PRODUCT AND GOVERNMENT EXPENDITURES: ALTERNATIVE SERIES FOR OECD COUNTRIES, VARYING YEARS, 1950–1974

| Year | Gross National Product | Net National Product | National Income | Government Expenditures | | | | | | |
| | | | | Total | External | | | Total | Domestic | |
					Total	Defense	Transfers		Transfers	Other
				AUSTRIA (series 1) (billion schillings)						
1960	161.29	145.43	125.04	49.85	2.01	1.89	.12	47.64	16.18	31.46
1961	177.47	159.90	136.69	55.81	2.00	1.89	.11	53.81	18.67	35.14
1962	188.27	168.18	143.75	62.40	2.15	2.07	.08	60.25	22.26	37.99
1963	202.78	180.78	154.88	69.54	2.99	2.60	.39	66.55	24.65	41.90
1964	221.15	197.25	167.86	78.23	3.79	3.40	.39	74.44	27.23	47.21
1965	241.22	214.77	182.44	83.52	3.50	2.95	.55	80.02	29.54	50.48
1966	262.09	233.49	197.27	91.58	3.92	3.47	.45	87.66	32.74	54.92
1967	279.13	248.64	210.25	102.97	4.12	3.62	.50	98.85	36.49	62.36
1968	295.10	262.90	218.90	112.30	4.10	3.70	.40	108.20	40.30	67.90
1969	323.30	288.70	240.70	...	...	...	...	...	...	...
				CANADA (million Canadian dollars)						
1961	37,435	32,922	28,161	12,083	1,802	1,746	56	10,281	3,441	6,840
1962	40,533	35,670	30,557	13,036	1,878	1,842	36	11,158	3,725	7,433
1963	43,385	38,218	32,773	13,673	1,780	1,715	65	11,893	3,848	8,045
1964	47,353	41,785	35,289	14,695	1,853	1,784	69	12,842	4,133	8,709
1965	52,146	46,069	38,784	16,172	1,783	1,690	93	14,389	4,574	9,815

Table B-2 (continued)

Year	Gross National Product	Net National Product	National Income	Government Expenditures Total	External Total	External Defense	External Transfers	Total	Domestic Transfers	Other
				CANADA (million Canadian dollars)—continued						
1966	58,017	51,430	43,132	18,660	2,027	1,861	166	16,633	5,047	11,586
1967	62,014	55,052	46,075	21,086	2,156	1,975	181	18,930	6,223	12,707
1968	67,297	60,076	50,458	23,260	2,098	1,965	133	21,162	7,194	13,968
				DENMARK (million kroner)						
1962	51,370	47,408	41,304	14,498	1,672	1,509	163	12,826	3,933	8,890
1963	54,647	50,201	43,206	15,708	1,768	1,577	191	13,940	4,396	9,540
1964	62,464	57,559	49,533	17,870	2,029	1,790	239	15,841	4,762	11,070
1965	70,162	64,597	55,334	21,137	2,202	1,882	320	18,935	5,802	13,130
1966	77,010	70,803	60,035	24,544	2,349	1,974	375	22,195	6,874	15,320
1967	84,374	77,595	65,582	29,030	2,764	2,342	422	26,266	8,308	17,950
1968	93,017	85,507	71,442	33,916	2,896	2,372	524	31,020	9,970	21,050
1969	106,349	98,078	81,528	38,790	3,078	2,466	612	35,712	11,371	24,340
1970	117,806	108,447	89,723	47,214	3,431	2,736	695	43,783	13,532	30,250
1971	128,618	118,274	98,069	54,646	4,063	3,108	955	50,583	15,377	35,200

FRANCE (series 1)
(billion francs)

Year										
1960	301.58	275.06	231.03	98.09	21.37	16.40	4.97	76.72	38.95	37.77
1961	328.33	298.40	250.87	110.54	25.85	20.40	5.45	84.69	44.50	40.19
1962	367.17	333.04	280.00	128.36	27.54	22.18	5.36	100.82	53.45	47.37
1963	411.99	372.44	312.18	146.72	27.71	22.85	4.86	119.01	63.50	55.51
1964	456.67	411.87	343.49	162.68	29.52	24.28	5.24	133.16	71.49	61.67
1965	489.83	439.96	367.92	176.84	30.62	25.30	5.32	146.22	78.80	67.42
1966	532.54	477.14	399.06	191.27	32.16	26.73	5.43	159.11	86.35	72.76
1967	573.23	511.56	430.00	210.10	34.89	28.91	5.98	175.21	94.59	80.62
1968	628.52	560.68	478.15	236.39	36.37	30.26	6.11	200.02	104.64	95.38
1969	725.64	647.89	549.02	266.49	37.44	30.70	6.74	229.05	121.74	107.31

FRANCE (series 2)
(billion francs)

Year										
1970	809.17	724.37	619.67	295.46	41.35	32.67	8.68	254.11	135.15	118.96
1971	899.62	804.29	689.09	329.29	46.50	34.91	11.59	282.79	151.40	131.39
1972	1,001.94	895.03	768.36	369.14	51.20	37.99	13.21	317.94	172.17	145.77

FEDERAL REPUBLIC OF GERMANY (series 1)
(billion DM)

Year										
1960	296.8	270.56	229.80	93.44	11.42	9.41	2.01	82.02	37.42	44.60
1961	326.2	296.55	251.60	105.30	14.00	11.46	2.54	91.30	40.99	50.31
1962	354.5	320.67	271.90	119.57	17.59	14.94	2.65	101.98	44.89	57.09
1963	377.6	339.80	289.04	131.75	20.04	17.33	2.71	111.71	47.86	63.85
1964	413.8	371.84	316.50	142.34	18.64	15.98	2.66	123.70	52.73	70.97
1965	452.7	405.62	345.43	158.23	20.78	18.00	2.78	137.45	58.97	78.48

Table B-2 (continued)

Year	Gross National Product	Net National Product	National Income	Government Expenditures						
					External				Domestic	
				Total	Total	Defense	Transfers	Total	Transfers	Other

FEDERAL REPUBLIC OF GERMANY (series 1; billion DM)—continued

Year	GNP	NNP	NI	Total	Total	Defense	Transfers	Total	Transfers	Other
1966	480.8	428.60	364.75	170.16	20.22	17.86	2.36	149.94	64.40	85.54
1967	485.1	430.08	363.68	181.97	21.40	18.60	2.80	160.57	70.88	89.69
1968	528.8	469.50	402.46	193.42	21.07	16.50	4.57	172.35	74.90	97.45

LUXEMBOURG (million francs)

Year	GNP	NNP	NI	Total	Total	Defense	Transfers	Total	Transfers	Other
1968	39,273	32,580	29,752	16,872	588	374	214	16,284	8,351	7,933
1969	45,478	37,715	34,259	17,678	773	391	382	16,905	8,997	7,908
1970	53,084	44,544	40,407	19,644	905	416	489	18,739	9,965	8,774
1971	54,154	45,934	40,692	22,313	824	442	382	21,489	11,241	10,248
1972	60,113	51,313	45,781	25,782	777	517	260	25,005	13,262	11,743
1973	71,236	...	...	30,870	...	601	...	...	15,359	...
1974	...	...	...	...	...	710	...	...	...	...

NETHERLANDS (million guilders)

Year	GNP	NNP	NI	Total	Total	Defense	Transfers	Total	Transfers	Other
1968	91,678	83,878	74,368	40,160	3,300	3,070	230	36,860	15,080	21,780
1969	103,822	95,152	85,242	45,410	3,540	3,300	240	41,870	17,820	24,050
1970	115,840	...	...	...	...	...	...	...	...	...
1971	130,210									

NORWAY
(million kroner)

Year										
1968	64,614	56,206	49,283	25,521	2,375	2,209	166	23,146	7,357	15,789
1969	70,172	61,280	53,493	29,278	2,693	2,448	245	26,585	8,491	18,094
1970	81,082	70,958	59,636	34,935	...	...	299	...	11,294	...
1971	90,951	79,414	66,634	40,711	...	...	347	...	13,562	...

SWEDEN
(million kroner)

Year										
1950	29,940	⋮	⋮	7,074	1,183	1,113	70	5,891	1,989	3,902
1951	36,623	⋮	⋮	8,095	1,413	1,443	−30	6,682	2,186	4,496
1952	40,348	⋮	⋮	9,623	1,750	1,782	−32	7,873	2,341	5,532
1953	41,375	⋮	⋮	10,467	2,019	1,995	24	8,448	2,700	5,748
1954	44,084	⋮	⋮	11,160	2,159	2,132	27	9,001	2,984	6,017
1955	47,367	⋮	⋮	12,299	2,230	2,203	27	10,069	3,420	6,649
1956	51,479	⋮	⋮	13,722	2,437	2,406	31	11,285	3,770	7,515
1957	55,460	⋮	⋮	15,235	2,611	2,559	52	12,624	4,154	8,470
1958	58,248	⋮	⋮	16,728	2,721	2,686	35	14,007	4,730	9,277
1959	62,019	⋮	⋮	17,638	2,882	2,822	60	14,756	4,953	9,803
1960	67,386	⋮	⋮	19,289	3,045	2,974	71	16,244	5,520	10,724
1961	73,675	⋮	⋮	20,976	3,130	3,017	113	17,846	6,026	11,820
1962	79,792	⋮	⋮	23,648	3,781	3,626	155	19,867	6,788	13,079
1963	86,740	⋮	⋮	26,523	3,984	3,798	186	22,539	7,963	14,576
1964	96,587	⋮	⋮	29,541	4,298	4,064	234	25,243	9,038	16,205
1965	106,509	⋮	⋮	33,888	4,646	4,377	269	29,242	10,636	18,606
1966	116,159	⋮	⋮	39,025	5,253	4,928	325	33,772	12,125	21,647
1967	124,884	⋮	⋮	44,138	5,154	4,734	420	38,984	14,232	24,752
1968	132,292	⋮	⋮	49,476	5,668	5,215	453	43,808	16,109	27,699

Table B-2 (continued)

| Year | Gross National Product | Net National Product | National Income | Government Expenditures | | | | | |
| | | | | External | | | Total | Domestic | |
				Total	Defense	Transfers		Transfers	Other
				SWITZERLAND					
				(million francs)					
1968	74,220	66,320	61,850	3,425	1,615	1,810	15,740	4,150	11,590
1969	80,930	72,230	67,130	3,840	1,775	2,065	17,965	5,370	12,595
1970	88,855	...	...	...	...	...	...	...	...
1971	100,765	...	...	...	...	...	...	...	...
1972	116,070	...	...	...	...	...	...	...	...
1973	129,380	...	...	...	...	...	...	...	...
				UNITED KINGDOM					
				(million pounds sterling)					
1960	25,773	23,840	20,936	1,677	1,583	94	6,625	1,569	5,056
1961	27,529	25,464	22,407	1,801	1,683	118	7,284	1,712	5,572
1962	28,921	26,724	23,428	1,925	1,804	121	7,809	1,885	5,924
1963	30,715	28,397	24,910	1,981	1,849	132	8,400	2,133	6,267
1964	33,321	30,829	26,880	2,091	1,928	163	9,076	2,257	6,819
1965	35,827	33,130	28,707	2,239	2,062	177	10,039	2,604	7,435
1966	38,153	35,216	30,160	2,330	2,150	180	11,015	2,834	8,181
1967	40,146	36,997	31,788	2,523	2,335	188	12,524	3,199	9,325
1968	43,009	39,631	33,577	2,549	2,370	179	13,953	3,690	10,263
1969	45,765	42,071	35,047	2,442	2,267	175	14,829	3,930	10,899

UNITED STATES

(million dollars)

Year										
1968	879,495	794,093	716,627	279,914	82,993	80,873	2,120	196,921	54,069	142,852
1969	946,871	853,666	772,232	298,473	83,407	81,355	2,052	215,066	59,585	155,481
1970	1,004,140	894,928	806,711	334,222	80,175	77,978	2,197	254,047	72,305	181,742
1971	1,085,052	967,502	866,629	363,190	78,000	75,412	2,588	285,190	85,579	199,611
1972	1,186,021	1,059,357	939,716	394,319	81,603	78,740	2,863	312,716	94,558	218,158

Note: The series given here are the following: *Austria:* 1960–1968, series 1, former SNA. *Canada:* 1960–1968, former SNA. *Denmark:* 1962–1971, former SNA. *France:* 1960–1969, series 1, former SNA; 1970–1972, series 2, former SNA. *Federal Republic of Germany:* 1960–1968, series 1, former SNA. *Luxembourg:* 1968–1973, present SNA. *Netherlands:* 1968–1969, former SNA. *Norway:* 1968–1971, former SNA. *Sweden:* 1950–1968, former SNA. *Switzerland:* 1968–1969, series 1, former SNA. *United Kingdom:* 1960–1969, former SNA. *United States:* 1968–1972, former SNA.

Ellipsis (. . .): not available.

Source: Table A-2.

Table B-3

GOVERNMENT EXPENDITURES AS A PERCENTAGE OF NATIONAL INCOME: OECD COUNTRIES, 1950–1974

Year	Total Expenditures	External Expenditures			Domestic Expenditures		
		Total	Defense	Transfers	Total	Transfers	Other
1960	28.59	3.57	3.12	.45	25.02	7.16	17.86
			A U S T R A L I A				
1961	30.65	3.89	3.35	.55	26.76	7.69	19.07
1962	30.30	3.76	3.20	.57	26.54	7.44	19.10
1963	30.00	3.70	3.09	.61	26.30	7.38	18.92
1964	30.41	4.11	3.43	.68	26.30	7.08	19.22
1965	32.97	5.19	4.41	.78	27.78	7.28	20.50
1966	33.00	5.49	4.65	.84	27.51	7.13	20.37
1967	34.06	5.91	5.11	.80	28.15	7.05	21.11
1968	32.87	5.44	4.71	.74	27.42	6.80	20.63
1969	32.61	4.86	4.11	.75	27.74	6.98	20.77
1970	33.23	4.74	4.03	.70	28.49	7.02	21.47
1971	33.82	4.42	3.72	.70	29.40	7.33	22.07
1972	33.74	4.15	3.41	.74	29.58	7.95	21.64
1973	33.22	3.89	3.19	.70	29.33	8.02	21.32
1974	38.92	3.71	2.98	.73	35.22	9.65	25.57
			A U S T R I A				
1950	30.85	.92	.89	.02	29.93	9.66	20.28

Year							
1951	34.56	1.11	1.09	.02	33.45	10.49	22.96
1952	36.42	.75	.75	—	35.68	12.45	23.22
1953	37.57	.68	.68	—	36.88	13.40	23.49
1954	35.22	.04	—	.04	35.18	12.64	22.55
1955	35.18	.24	.23	.01	34.94	11.99	22.94
1956	37.66	1.16	1.15	.01	36.50	12.56	23.95
1957	38.56	1.79	1.67	.12	36.78	12.85	23.93
1958	41.13	2.02	1.86	.16	39.11	13.43	25.67
1959	41.59	1.86	1.80	.06	39.73	13.86	25.87
1960	39.40	1.61	1.50	.10	37.79	13.49	24.30
1961	40.25	1.44	1.36	.08	38.81	14.07	24.73
1962	42.22	1.46	1.40	.05	40.77	15.36	25.40
1963	43.73	1.97	1.64	.33	41.76	15.83	25.93
1964	44.73	2.29	1.97	.32	42.45	15.95	26.49
1965	44.49	1.86	1.57	.29	42.63	16.04	26.59
1966	45.48	1.94	1.72	.22	43.53	16.55	26.99
1967	47.97	1.93	1.69	.24	46.04	17.42	28.62
1968	49.12	1.84	1.64	.20	47.28	17.97	29.31
1969	48.40	1.78	1.59	.19	46.62	17.87	28.75
1970	47.65	1.66	1.47	.19	45.99	17.28	28.72
1971	48.47	1.55	1.34	.20	46.92	17.74	29.18
1972	48.82	1.57	1.36	.21	47.26	17.68	29.58
1973	49.20	1.54	1.30	.24	47.67	17.31	30.35

BELGIUM

Year							
1953	31.78	5.78	5.69	.09	26.01	12.33	13.67
1954	31.27	5.21	5.07	.14	26.06	11.76	14.30
1955	29.83	4.23	4.09	.13	25.60	11.52	14.08

Table B-3 (continued)

Year	Total Expenditures	External Expenditures			Domestic Expenditures		
		Total	Defense	Transfers	Total	Transfers	Other
			BELGIUM (continued)				
1956	29.94	4.27	4.14	.13	25.67	11.29	14.38
1957	29.73	3.96	3.85	.12	25.77	11.25	14.52
1958	32.43	4.20	4.10	.09	28.24	12.75	15.48
1959	34.48	4.23	4.09	.14	30.25	13.83	16.41
1960	37.36	4.22	4.11	.11	33.14	13.99	19.15
1961	37.11	4.01	3.70	.31	33.10	13.71	19.38
1962	38.13	4.24	3.87	.37	33.90	14.15	19.75
1963	39.47	4.46	4.08	.38	35.01	14.36	20.65
1964	38.59	4.13	3.82	.31	34.47	13.63	20.84
1965	40.17	3.93	3.65	.28	36.23	15.46	20.78
1966	42.12	3.70	3.42	.28	38.42	16.07	22.35
1967	43.62	3.94	3.52	.42	39.69	16.44	23.25
1968	45.73	3.91	3.43	.47	41.82	17.67	24.15
1969	45.39	3.94	3.43	.51	41.45	17.21	24.24
1970	45.88	3.89	3.15	.74	41.99	17.69	24.30
1971	47.52	4.08	3.25	.83	43.44	17.87	25.57
1972	48.08	3.83	3.21	.62	44.25	18.45	25.80
1973	47.80	3.96	3.09	.87	43.84	18.91	24.93
1974	48.28	3.65	2.93	.72	44.63	19.54	25.09
			CANADA				
1950	28.32	4.15	4.11	.04	24.17	7.29	16.88

1951	30.20	8.09	8.04	.05	22.11	6.23	15.87
1952	33.54	10.40	10.32	.09	23.14	7.30	15.84
1953	34.45	10.55	10.42	.13	23.90	7.58	16.31
1954	36.07	9.77	9.71	.06	26.30	8.60	17.70
1955	35.16	9.15	9.04	.12	26.01	8.40	17.61
1956	34.57	8.38	8.25	.13	26.19	7.64	18.55
1957	36.20	7.87	7.70	.17	28.33	8.67	19.66
1958	38.86	7.20	6.98	.21	31.67	10.55	21.11
1959	39.13	6.45	6.17	.27	32.69	10.42	22.26
1960	41.13	6.30	6.07	.22	34.83	11.40	23.44
1961	41.17	6.07	5.81	.26	35.10	9.17	25.93
1962	40.91	5.82	5.64	.18	35.08	9.07	26.01
1963	40.17	5.23	4.97	.26	34.94	8.66	26.29
1964	39.57	5.10	4.85	.25	34.46	8.49	25.97
1965	40.20	4.35	4.06	.29	35.85	8.37	27.47
1966	41.39	4.27	3.85	.42	37.12	8.17	28.95
1967	44.02	4.42	3.98	.44	39.59	9.46	30.13
1968	45.00	3.88	3.56	.31	41.12	10.12	31.00
1969	45.17	3.48	3.17	.31	41.69	10.28	31.42
1970	48.70	3.62	3.24	.38	45.08	10.98	34.10
1971	50.04	3.41	3.05	.36	46.63	11.82	34.81
1972	50.31	3.21	2.85	.35	47.10	12.65	34.45
1973	48.47	2.98	2.64	.34	45.49	12.28	33.21
1974	51.27	3.05	2.68	.37	48.21	12.85	35.36

DENMARK

1950	22.85	1.97	1.81	.16	20.88	6.78	14.09
1951	25.65	2.90	2.77	.12	22.76	7.63	15.12
1952	26.81	3.39	3.26	.14	23.42	7.84	15.58
1953	27.01	3.88	3.75	.13	23.13	7.68	15.45
1954	27.68	4.24	4.09	.15	23.44	7.45	15.99
1955	28.87	4.00	3.81	.19	24.87	8.24	16.63

Table B-3 (continued)

Year	Total Expenditures	External Expenditures			Domestic Expenditures		
		Total	Defense	Transfers	Total	Transfers	Other
		DENMARK (continued)					
1956	30.53	3.91	3.65	.26	26.62	8.34	18.28
1957	31.36	3.64	3.37	.27	27.72	9.31	18.41
1958	32.15	3.67	3.35	.32	28.48	9.55	18.94
1959	31.22	3.43	3.11	.32	27.80	9.20	18.60
1960	31.13	3.53	3.16	.37	27.60	9.09	18.51
1961	33.74	3.63	3.24	.39	30.11	9.24	20.87
1962	34.75	4.08	3.68	.40	30.67	9.59	21.08
1963	36.08	4.12	3.68	.45	31.96	10.25	21.71
1964	35.75	4.13	3.64	.49	31.62	9.68	21.94
1965	37.87	4.01	3.42	.58	33.86	10.56	23.31
1966	40.55	3.94	3.31	.63	36.61	11.53	25.09
1967	43.95	4.25	3.60	.65	39.71	12.76	26.95
1968	47.19	4.09	3.35	.74	43.10	14.07	29.03
1969	47.19	3.80	3.05	.76	43.39	14.05	29.34
1970	52.55	3.85	3.05	.80	48.70	15.22	33.48
1971	55.98	4.04	3.12	.92	51.94	16.08	35.85
1972	55.53	3.89	2.93	.97	51.64	16.41	35.23
1973	54.36	3.95	2.76	1.19	50.41	16.57	33.84
1974	58.74	…	…	1.32	…	17.49	…
		FRANCE					
1950	37.27	8.20	7.58	.61	29.07	14.79	14.28

Year							
1951	39.23	8.06	7.50	.55	31.17	15.64	15.53
1952	43.28	9.97	9.18	.80	33.31	15.97	17.34
1953	44.40	11.42	10.61	.81	32.98	16.72	16.26
1954	42.65	8.83	8.05	.79	33.81	16.95	16.86
1955	42.37	7.39	6.45	.93	34.98	17.30	17.68
1956	44.89	9.45	8.28	1.17	35.44	17.38	18.06
1957	45.07	9.52	8.41	1.11	35.54	17.68	17.87
1958	43.60	8.55	7.38	1.17	35.05	17.34	17.71
1959	43.38	9.79	7.67	2.12	33.59	16.98	16.61
1960	43.20	9.41	7.22	2.19	33.79	17.16	16.63
1961	44.67	10.45	8.24	2.20	34.23	17.98	16.24
1962	46.28	9.93	8.00	1.93	36.35	19.27	17.08
1963	47.27	8.93	7.36	1.57	38.34	20.46	17.88
1964	47.48	8.62	7.09	1.53	38.86	20.87	18.00
1965	48.09	8.33	6.88	1.45	39.76	21.43	18.33
1966	47.84	8.04	6.69	1.36	39.80	21.60	18.20
1967	48.48	8.05	6.67	1.38	40.43	21.83	18.60
1968	49.02	7.55	6.27	1.29	41.47	21.79	19.67
1969	48.40	6.84	5.57	1.28	41.56	21.92	19.64
1970	50.04	6.76	5.55	1.21	43.28	22.98	20.30
1971	49.71	6.64	5.33	1.30	43.07	23.30	19.77
1972	49.61	6.50	5.16	1.34	43.11	23.70	19.41
1973	49.74	6.45	5.06	1.39	43.29	24.17	19.11
1974	50.27	6.14	4.91	1.23	44.13	24.17	19.96
1950	39.28	6.61	5.83	.78	32.66	16.02	16.64

FEDERAL REPUBLIC OF GERMANY

Table B-3 (continued)

Year	Total Expenditures	External Expenditures			Domestic Expenditures		
		Total	Defense	Transfers	Total	Transfers	Other
			FEDERAL REPUBLIC OF GERMANY (continued)				
1951	39.39	8.00	6.76	1.24	31.39	14.71	16.68
1952	41.03	8.74	7.25	1.49	32.29	15.18	17.11
1953	40.58	7.74	5.67	2.07	32.84	15.52	17.32
1954	39.66	6.98	4.92	2.06	32.68	15.16	17.53
1955	38.42	6.26	4.34	1.92	32.16	14.79	17.37
1956	38.35	5.48	3.55	1.93	32.87	14.91	17.96
1957	40.26	5.33	3.21	2.12	34.93	16.72	18.21
1958	42.03	5.54	3.35	2.19	36.49	17.59	18.90
1959	42.35	6.40	4.01	2.39	35.95	16.94	19.01
1960	40.27	4.96	4.09	.87	35.30	15.95	19.35
1961	41.15	5.49	4.45	1.04	35.66	15.90	19.76
1962	43.48	6.45	5.43	1.02	37.03	16.23	20.80
1963	44.94	6.80	5.83	.97	38.14	16.23	21.91
1964	44.55	5.77	4.89	.88	38.78	16.30	22.48
1965	45.46	5.87	4.99	.87	39.60	16.64	22.95
1966	46.22	5.40	4.71	.68	40.82	17.08	23.74
1967	49.00	5.74	4.93	.81	43.25	18.86	24.39
1968	47.26	5.20	4.03	1.17	42.07	17.84	24.23
1969	47.29	5.28	4.08	1.20	42.00	17.45	24.55
1970	46.57	4.73	3.75	.98	41.84	16.42	25.42
1971	48.11	5.05	4.02	1.03	43.06	16.58	26.48
1972	49.37	5.14	3.85	1.30	44.22	17.24	26.98
1973	50.19	5.19	3.78	1.41	45.00	17.27	27.74
1974	54.13	5.32	3.96	1.35	48.81	18.59	30.22

I T A L Y

Year						
1951	28.32	4.15	3.98	.17	24.17	7.79	16.38
1952	31.70	4.23	4.08	.15	27.47	9.59	17.88
1953	32.04	3.86	3.67	.19	28.18	10.19	17.98
1954	34.70	4.00	3.90	.10	30.70	11.25	19.44
1955	34.68	3.68	3.51	.17	30.99	11.65	19.34
1956	35.42	3.56	3.51	.05	31.86	12.40	19.46
1957	34.85	3.25	3.25	—	31.60	12.21	19.39
1958	35.65	3.25	3.22	.03	32.40	13.19	19.21
1959	36.65	3.19	3.10	.09	33.46	13.56	19.90
1960	36.91	3.23	3.13	.10	33.68	13.31	20.37
1961	35.34	3.00	2.96	.05	32.34	12.93	19.41
1962	36.41	3.08	2.99	.10	33.32	13.49	19.83
1963	37.52	3.15	3.05	.10	34.37	14.28	20.09
1964	38.33	3.01	2.94	.07	35.32	14.18	21.14
1965	41.27	3.21	3.10	.11	38.06	16.57	21.49
1966	41.36	3.13	3.03	.10	38.23	16.68	21.55
1967	40.71	2.88	2.72	.16	37.84	16.65	21.19
1968	42.50	3.00	2.76	.24	39.50	17.47	22.03
1969	41.92	2.75	2.62	.12	39.18	17.54	21.64
1970	41.35	3.02	2.49	.54	38.33	17.36	20.97
1971	46.11	3.64	2.84	.80	42.46	18.99	23.47
1972	48.01	3.65	2.85	.80	44.36	19.76	24.61
1973	48.51	3.49	2.53	.96	45.02	19.90	25.12

J A P A N

Year						
1952	17.18	...	...	—	...	3.00	...
1953	18.72	2.44	2.44	—	16.28	3.41	12.87
1954	19.51	2.41	2.40	.02	17.09	4.67	12.42
1955	18.80	2.12	1.99	.13	16.69	5.03	11.66

Table B-3 (continued)

Year	Total Expenditures	External Expenditures			Domestic Expenditures		
		Total	Defense	Transfers	Total	Transfers	Other
			JAPAN (continued)				
1956	17.35	1.82	1.69	.13	15.53	4.50	11.03
1957	16.49	1.95	1.62	.33	14.54	4.05	10.49
1958	18.33	2.58	1.60	.98	15.75	4.72	11.03
1959	17.53	1.76	1.48	.28	15.77	4.93	10.84
1960	22.37	1.51	1.28	.23	20.86	4.64	16.22
1961	21.37	1.39	1.15	.24	19.98	4.29	15.69
1962	23.40	1.40	1.22	.18	22.00	4.65	17.35
1963	23.89	1.36	1.21	.16	22.53	4.94	17.59
1964	23.56	1.30	1.17	.13	22.26	4.98	17.27
1965	24.81	1.30	1.17	.13	23.51	5.51	18.01
1966	25.14	1.30	1.14	.16	23.84	5.54	18.30
1967	23.79	1.23	1.06	.16	22.56	5.35	17.21
1968	23.82	1.15	1.01	.14	22.68	5.23	17.44
1969	23.99	1.13	1.01	.13	22.86	5.20	17.65
1970	24.05	1.11	1.00	.11	22.94	5.37	17.58
1971	25.70	1.17	1.04	.12	24.53	5.45	19.09
1972	27.21	1.21	1.07	.14	26.00	5.92	20.09
1973	26.76	1.11	1.05	.07	25.64	5.90	19.74
1974	29.26	1.05	.99	.06	28.21	6.95	21.27

LUXEMBOURG

Year							
1952	28.99	2.69	2.46	.23	26.30	9.86	16.44
1953	34.24	3.44	3.17	.27	30.80	11.90	18.90
1954	35.37	3.91	3.85	.06	31.45	13.18	18.28
1955	34.85	3.23	3.18	.05	31.63	13.47	18.15
1956	31.70	2.87	2.82	.04	28.83	13.28	15.55
1957	32.35	2.38	2.33	.05	29.97	13.93	16.04
1958	36.94	2.49	2.42	.07	34.45	15.47	18.98
1959	46.48	1.79	1.70	.09	44.69	15.91	28.78
1960	39.24	1.58	1.40	.18	37.66	14.95	22.72
1961	38.68	1.61	1.45	.16	37.07	15.08	21.99
1962	42.22	1.93	1.75	.18	40.29	15.47	24.82
1963	42.41	1.81	1.61	.20	40.60	15.54	25.07
1964	41.60	2.02	1.85	.17	39.58	15.89	23.69
1965	43.67	2.05	1.86	.19	41.62	17.71	23.91
1966	45.91	2.17	1.85	.31	43.74	18.46	25.28
1967	49.82	2.05	1.53	.52	47.77	20.92	26.86
1968	50.05	2.01	1.28	.73	48.04	20.41	27.63
1969	46.14	2.32	1.17	1.15	43.82	19.55	24.27
1970	43.58	2.36	1.08	1.27	41.23	18.41	22.82
1971	46.85	2.04	1.09	.95	44.82	20.32	24.50
1972	50.85	1.77	1.18	.59	49.08	21.54	27.54
1973	...	...	...	...	...	...	...
1974	...	...	...	...	...	...	...

NETHERLANDS

Year							
1950	34.07	6.12	6.04	.08	27.95	8.44	19.51
1951	34.62	6.34	6.27	.08	28.28	8.69	19.59
1952	34.57	7.15	7.08	.06	27.42	9.30	18.12
1953	36.55	7.02	6.96	.06	29.53	9.29	20.24
1954	35.96	7.48	7.34	.14	28.48	9.21	19.27
1955	35.39	7.31	6.93	.39	28.08	8.77	19.30

Table B-3 (continued)

NETHERLANDS (continued)

Year	Total Expenditures	External Expenditures			Domestic Expenditures		
		Total	Defense	Transfers	Total	Transfers	Other
1956	39.75	7.25	6.96	.29	32.49	8.92	23.57
1957	43.14	6.76	6.48	.28	36.39	10.87	25.51
1958	43.69	5.68	5.38	.30	38.01	12.65	25.36
1959	41.82	4.71	4.44	.27	37.11	12.37	24.74
1960	41.65	4.87	4.69	.18	36.77	12.42	24.36
1961	42.43	5.25	4.89	.35	37.18	12.75	24.43
1962	43.81	5.43	4.91	.51	38.39	13.46	24.93
1963	46.33	5.25	5.30	—.05	41.08	15.40	25.68
1964	47.19	5.29	5.04	.25	41.90	15.39	26.51
1965	48.69	4.85	4.52	.33	43.84	16.88	26.96
1966	51.54	4.65	4.38	.28	46.89	18.41	28.47
1967	53.50	4.91	4.49	.42	48.58	19.30	29.28
1968	52.13	4.60	4.21	.39	47.52	21.17	26.35
1969	52.05	4.22	3.91	.31	47.83	21.74	26.09
1970	54.34	4.46	4.14	.31	49.89	22.79	27.10
1971	57.65	5.43	4.26	1.17	52.22	24.68	27.54
1972	58.35	5.19	3.99	1.20	53.16	26.05	27.11
1973	58.52	5.18	3.80	1.38	53.34	26.71	26.62
1974	61.02	5.05	3.74	1.31	55.97	29.01	26.96

1951	30.19	3.75	3.64	.11	26.44	6.04	20.40
1952	33.10	4.96	4.84	.12	28.13	6.82	21.31
1953	35.78	5.98	5.80	.18	29.80	7.50	22.30
1954	35.53	5.92	5.74	.17	29.61	7.85	21.77
1955	35.25	4.67	4.58	.10	30.58	8.15	22.42
1956	34.95	4.37	4.28	.09	30.58	7.97	22.61
1957	37.32	4.46	4.36	.10	32.86	8.87	24.00
1958	40.14	4.50	4.41	.09	35.64	10.00	25.64
1959	42.06	4.56	4.47	.09	37.50	11.24	26.26
1960	41.77	4.28	4.15	.13	37.49	11.04	26.45
1961	41.60	4.25	4.10	.14	37.35	11.09	26.27
1962	44.14	4.58	4.43	.15	39.56	12.05	27.51
1963	45.66	4.57	4.36	.22	41.09	12.43	28.66
1964	45.75	4.49	4.26	.23	41.25	12.68	28.57
1965	47.31	4.93	4.70	.24	42.37	12.72	29.65
1966	48.03	4.68	4.41	.27	43.35	13.08	30.27
1967	49.89	4.62	4.38	.23	45.28	13.88	31.40
1968	50.60	5.25	4.91	.35	45.35	15.35	30.00
1969	53.18	5.35	4.92	.43	47.83	16.35	31.48
1970	57.12	5.40	4.88	.52	51.72	19.34	32.38
1971	60.62	5.16	4.73	.43	55.47	21.20	34.26
1972	62.42	5.07	4.53	.54	57.34	22.05	35.29
1973	62.29	4.88	4.32	.56	57.41	22.51	34.90
1974	62.88	4.89	4.18	.71	57.99	21.88	36.11

Table B-3 (continued)

Year	Total Expenditures	External Expenditures			Domestic Expenditures		
		Total	Defense	Transfers	Total	Transfers	Other
			S W E D E N				
1960	38.46	5.12	5.04	.08	33.34	10.41	22.94
1961	38.64	4.80	4.72	.08	33.84	10.44	23.40
1962	40.71	5.45	5.33	.12	35.26	10.78	24.48
1963	43.34	5.60	5.41	.19	37.74	11.52	26.23
1964	43.38	5.37	5.19	.18	38.01	11.48	26.53
1965	45.05	5.28	5.10	.18	39.76	12.27	27.50
1966	47.96	5.55	5.29	.26	42.41	12.80	29.61
1967	50.56	5.12	4.79	.34	45.44	13.75	31.69
1968	53.45	5.30	4.92	.37	48.15	14.65	33.50
1969	53.28	5.22	4.67	.55	48.06	15.05	33.00
1970	54.21	4.79	4.33	.45	49.42	15.14	34.29
1971	58.45	5.30	4.82	.48	53.14	17.18	35.96
1972	60.15	4.98	4.41	.57	55.17	18.18	36.99
1973	59.60	5.09	4.53	.56	54.51	18.40	36.10
1974	63.58	...	...	.78	...	21.54	...
			S W I T Z E R L A N D				
1950	22.06	2.90	2.78	.12	19.16	5.62	13.54

Year							
1951	21.98	3.47	3.34	.13	18.51	5.69	12.81
1952	23.12	4.27	4.22	.05	18.85	5.94	12.91
1953	22.07	3.61	3.51	.10	18.47	5.86	12.61
1954	21.56	2.98	2.89	.09	18.58	6.19	12.39
1955	21.26	3.10	2.97	.13	18.16	6.09	12.07
1956	21.23	2.64	2.50	.14	18.59	6.51	12.08
1957	22.82	3.52	3.31	.21	19.30	6.86	12.44
1958	24.23	3.66	3.46	.20	20.57	7.23	13.34
1959	23.11	3.32	3.10	.22	19.79	7.13	12.66
1960	24.42	5.51	2.72	2.80	18.91	4.63	14.27
1961	25.83	5.67	2.92	2.75	20.16	4.95	15.21
1962	27.19	5.88	3.04	2.84	21.31	5.09	16.22
1963	28.30	5.69	3.04	2.66	22.60	5.04	17.56
1964	29.86	5.48	3.01	2.47	24.38	6.13	18.25
1965	29.69	5.49	2.93	2.56	24.20	6.21	17.99
1966	30.72	5.99	2.99	3.00	24.73	6.34	18.39
1967	31.28	5.88	2.83	3.05	25.40	6.86	18.54
1968	26.65	:	:	.31	:	11.05	:
1969	28.09	:	:	.42	:	12.36	:
1970	27.53	:	:	.39	:	12.03	:
1971	28.13	:	:	.39	:	12.07	:
1972	27.88	:	:	.41	:	11.65	:
1973	30.30	:	:	.51	:	13.72	:
1974	31.57	:	:	.52	:	14.17	:

UNITED KINGDOM

Year							
1950	39.12	8.02	7.55	.47	31.09	6.45	24.65
1951	42.58	9.62	9.07	.55	32.97	6.08	26.89
1952	45.31	11.82	11.28	.54	33.48	6.55	26.93
1953	43.92	11.56	11.05	.50	32.37	6.73	25.64
1954	40.99	10.87	10.39	.48	30.11	6.48	23.63
1955	39.57	9.89	9.44	.45	29.67	6.67	23.00

Table B-3 (continued)

Year	Total Expenditures	External Expenditures			Domestic Expenditures		
		Total	Defense	Transfers	Total	Transfers	Other
		UNITED KINGDOM (continued)					
1956	39.45	9.60	9.16	.43	29.85	6.56	23.29
1957	38.81	8.93	8.51	.42	29.88	6.54	23.34
1958	39.24	8.26	7.85	.41	30.98	7.53	23.45
1959	39.65	8.13	7.71	.42	31.52	7.93	23.60
1960	39.42	8.10	7.67	.43	31.32	7.57	23.75
1961	41.36	8.13	7.64	.49	33.23	8.74	24.50
1962	42.51	8.29	7.81	.47	34.22	9.21	25.02
1963	42.53	8.00	7.51	.48	34.53	9.71	24.82
1964	42.14	7.78	7.22	.56	34.36	9.47	24.90
1965	43.44	7.78	7.22	.56	35.66	10.14	25.52
1966	44.79	7.66	7.13	.54	37.12	10.50	26.62
1967	47.89	7.87	7.35	.52	40.03	11.20	28.83
1968	49.22	7.40	6.95	.46	41.81	12.02	29.79
1969	49.13	6.73	6.30	.43	42.40	12.27	30.13
1970	49.29	6.55	6.16	.38	42.74	12.32	30.42
1971	48.41	6.55	6.14	.40	41.87	12.11	29.76
1972	50.07	6.46	6.10	.36	43.61	13.20	30.41
1973	49.95	6.37	5.80	.57	43.58	12.62	30.96
1974	55.25	6.73	6.31	.42	48.52	13.40	35.12

1950	26.28	7.43	5.88	1.54	18.85	5.77	13.08
1951	29.64	13.19	12.02	1.17	16.45	4.02	12.44
1952	33.26	16.45	15.71	.74	16.81	3.83	12.98
1953	34.25	16.57	15.89	.68	17.68	3.93	13.75
1954	33.00	14.09	13.62	.48	18.90	4.67	14.23
1955	30.71	12.38	11.92	.46	18.32	4.62	13.71
1956	30.79	12.17	11.67	.51	18.61	4.66	13.95
1957	32.64	12.58	12.11	.47	20.06	5.24	14.82
1958	36.02	13.02	12.52	.50	23.01	6.34	16.67
1959	34.00	12.10	11.63	.47	21.90	6.03	15.87
1960	34.49	11.47	11.02	.46	23.01	6.21	16.80
1961	36.54	11.88	11.39	.49	24.66	6.89	17.77
1962	36.50	11.97	11.50	.47	24.53	6.59	17.94
1963	36.16	11.25	10.80	.45	24.91	6.59	18.32
1964	35.45	10.36	9.94	.42	25.10	6.34	18.76
1965	34.11	9.57	9.19	.38	24.54	6.30	18.24
1966	35.00	10.48	10.11	.36	24.52	6.32	18.20
1967	38.25	11.66	11.32	.34	26.59	7.13	19.46
1968	39.29	11.75	10.75	1.00	27.54	7.66	19.88
1969	39.03	11.03	10.38	.65	28.00	7.88	20.12
1970	41.95	10.17	9.57	.61	31.78	9.17	22.61
1971	42.00	9.13	8.45	.68	32.87	10.06	22.80
1972	41.51	8.75	8.00	.75	32.76	10.12	22.64
1973	40.20	7.79	7.26	.52	32.41	10.31	22.10
1974	. . .	. . .	. . .	. . .	. . .	. . .	. . .

Ellipsis (. . .): not available.
Dash (—): less than half a unit.
Source: Derived from Table B-1.

73

Table B-4

GOVERNMENT EXPENDITURES AS A PERCENTAGE OF NATIONAL INCOME: DEPARTMENT OF COMMERCE DATA FOR THE UNITED STATES, 1929–1976

Year	Total Expenditures	External Expenditures			Domestic Expenditures		
		Total[a]	Defense[b]	Transfers[c]	Total[d]	Transfer[e]	Other[f]
1929	12.12	.88	.84	.04	11.23	1.08	10.15
1930	15.00	1.04	.99	.05	13.96	1.37	12.59
1931	21.08	1.29	1.22	.07	19.79	3.54	16.25
1932	25.09	1.64	1.59	.05	23.45	3.40	20.05
1933	26.86	1.53	1.49	.04	25.33	3.68	21.65
1934	26.43	1.31	1.29	.02	25.13	3.21	21.91
1935	23.70	1.47	1.44	.04	22.23	3.22	19.01
1936	24.99	1.49	1.44	.05	23.50	4.57	18.93
1937	20.80	1.44	1.36	.08	19.36	2.58	16.78
1938	25.44	1.64	1.59	.04	23.80	3.66	20.14
1939	24.63	1.77	1.73	.04	22.86	3.54	19.32
1940	23.12	2.80	2.76	.04	20.32	3.39	16.94
1941	28.03	13.38	13.39	−.01	14.65	2.56	12.10
1942	47.16	36.44	36.37	.07	10.72	1.95	8.77
1943	55.15	47.11	47.14	−.03	8.04	1.45	6.59
1944	56.61	48.01	48.06	−.05	8.61	1.69	6.91
1945	51.33	40.89	40.70	.19	10.44	3.12	7.32
1946	25.56	9.55	8.29	1.26	16.01	6.08	9.93
1947	21.86	5.65	4.65	1.00	16.21	5.73	10.48
1948	23.05	6.62	4.87	1.75	16.43	4.85	11.58
1949	27.89	8.60	6.20	2.40	19.28	5.51	13.77

Year							
1950	25.82	7.43	5.92	1.51	18.39	6.10	12.29
1951	29.07	13.44	12.30	1.14	15.64	4.28	11.36
1952	32.85	16.77	16.04	.73	16.08	4.23	11.85
1953	33.88	16.87	16.21	.66	17.01	4.30	12.70
1954	32.43	14.34	13.74	.59	18.10	5.05	13.05
1955	29.86	12.34	11.72	.62	17.52	4.95	12.57
1956	30.11	12.11	11.58	.54	18.00	4.99	13.01
1957	31.81	12.64	12.15	.49	19.17	5.54	13.63
1958	35.05	13.01	12.52	.49	22.04	6.69	15.36
1959	32.99	11.95	11.48	.47	21.04	6.35	14.69
1960	33.11	11.25	10.79	.46	21.86	6.55	15.31
1961	35.14	11.57	11.08	.49	23.57	7.26	16.31
1962	35.09	11.63	11.16	.47	23.45	6.91	16.54
1963	34.75	10.87	10.42	.45	23.88	6.92	16.96
1964	33.95	9.86	9.45	.42	24.09	6.70	17.39
1965	33.19	9.12	8.74	.38	24.07	6.64	17.42
1966	34.32	10.06	9.70	.37	24.26	6.69	17.57
1967	36.97	11.24	10.90	.34	25.73	7.54	18.18
1968	37.64	11.06	10.76	.30	26.58	7.91	18.67
1969	37.20	10.20	9.93	.27	27.00	8.16	18.84
1970	39.07	9.49	9.21	.28	29.58	9.51	20.08
1971	39.68	8.49	8.18	.30	31.20	10.47	20.73
1972	38.96	8.01	7.72	.29	30.95	10.44	20.51
1973	38.03	7.15	6.91	.25	30.88	10.66	20.22
1974	40.34	7.06	6.78	.28	33.28	11.88	21.40
1975g	43.74	7.15	6.90	.25	36.59	13.95	22.63
1976g	41.90	6.60	6.36	.24	35.30	13.54	21.75

Table B-4 (continued)

a Sum of defense expenditures and external transfers.
b Entitled "government purchases of goods and services, national defense" in source, Table 3.1.
c Entitled "transfer payments to foreigners" in source, Table 1.1.
d Total expenditures minus total external expenditures.
e Entitled "transfer payments to persons" in source, Table 3.1.
f Total domestic expenditures minus domestic transfers.
g Preliminary data subject to later revision.

Source: Derived from data in U.S. Department of Commerce, *The National Income and Product Accounts of the United States, 1929–1974,* Tables 1.1, 1.9, and 3.1; *Survey of Current Business,* July 1977, same tables; and, for defense expenditures for 1929–1938, Solomon Fabricant, *The Trend of Government Activity in the United States since 1900* (New York: National Bureau of Economic Research, 1952), pp. 240–241. The data on defense expenditures last mentioned are given by Fabricant for fiscal years. They have been converted into estimates for calendar years through linear interpolation.

Table B-5

CENTRAL GOVERNMENT EXPENDITURES AS A PERCENTAGE OF TOTAL GOVERNMENT EXPENDITURES: OECD COUNTRIES, VARYING YEARS, 1950–1974

Year	Australia: Present SNA	Austria: Former SNA		Canada		Denmark: Former SNA	France (series 2)	
		Series 1	Series 2	Former SNA	Present SNA		Former SNA	Present SNA
1950		51.98		55.79			57.86	
1951		55.29		60.14			57.16	
1952		55.06		66.59			56.79	
1953		54.01		66.67			55.39	
1954		53.62		63.70			53.43	
1955		51.57		61.70			53.01	
1956		51.49		59.87			52.15	
1957		52.70		57.72			54.79	
1958		54.68		56.79		61.01	53.17	
1959		54.82		56.45		59.07	52.49	
1960	68.24	53.33		54.71	59.19	59.45		
1961	68.92	53.27		54.19	58.84	57.13		
1962	67.96	53.27	51.81	53.00	56.57	58.99		
1963	66.97	53.70	52.23	51.09	54.34	62.12		
1964	66.09	54.17	52.93	50.53	53.44	60.91		
1965	67.24	51.98	51.14	49.10	51.41	59.01		
1966	68.27	51.54	50.99	49.15	50.92	59.44		
1967	68.47	51.96	50.51	48.92	50.23	58.82		
1968	68.07	52.09	50.48	48.93	49.87	59.12		
1969	67.91		49.45		49.35	60.11		

Table B-5 (continued)

Year	Australia: Present SNA	Austria: Former SNA		Canada		Denmark: Former SNA	France (series 2)		Netherlands: Former SNA
		Series 1	Series 2	Former SNA	Present SNA		Former SNA	Present SNA	
1970	68.95		50.63		48.88		51.80	57.70	
1971	66.86		49.52		49.21		51.36	57.09	
1972	67.35		49.73		50.47		51.22	57.40	
1973	67.63		48.49		50.11			55.46	29.90
1974	69.62				52.17			57.78	27.89

Year	Federal Republic of Germany (series 1): Former SNA	Italy: Former SNA	Japan: Former SNA	Luxembourg	
				Former SNA	Present SNA
1950	34.45				
1951	45.51	62.91			
1952	46.24	63.03		69.82	
1953	44.90	62.94		70.48	
1954	43.54	61.01		69.97	
1955	40.76	59.75		62.45	
1956	39.24	58.68		60.85	
1957	38.15	54.69		60.99	
1958	37.23	54.60	45.39	61.99	
1959	37.99	55.00	43.44	48.20	
1960	36.27	54.47	40.95	50.24	
1961	36.58	53.08	42.87	53.76	
1962	37.37	55.62	42.12	52.43	
1963	37.03	53.14	44.94	53.45	
1964	36.13	53.45	45.19	53.57	

Year	Norway		Sweden		United Kingdom		United States	
	Former SNA	Present SNA	Former SNA	Present SNA	Former SNA	Present SNA	Former SNA	Present SNA
1950					76.36		56.66	
1951	70.77				78.05		66.51	
1952	70.96				76.63		69.79	
1953	71.46				75.41		69.70	
1954	70.74				74.87		63.46	
1955	69.15				74.07		60.40	
1956	69.83		73.39		74.03		59.45	
1957	70.95		75.54		73.93		58.58	
1958	69.56		75.67		72.56		57.45	
1959	72.16		77.47		72.63		57.01	
1960	72.17		73.97	58.27		73.07	54.59	
1961	72.48		73.00	57.14		71.75	53.82	
1962	72.15		74.09	57.38		70.44	54.95	
1963	71.87		71.26	55.85		68.57	54.01	
1964	71.71		74.12	54.23		67.43	54.07	
1965		36.62	54.48	46.07		50.00		25.35
1966		35.14	54.92	46.27		52.71		22.28
1967		34.99	51.07	45.92		51.21		18.92
1968		31.65	53.41			51.13	52.39	19.47
1969			54.72			49.67	50.21	18.56
1970			53.44			49.85	50.64	
1971			55.02			48.49	49.82	
1972			53.49			46.26	51.05	
1973			57.22				49.53	

Table B-5 (continued)

Year	Norway		Sweden		United Kingdom		United States	
	Former SNA	Present SNA	Former SNA	Present SNA	Former SNA	Present SNA	Former SNA	Present SNA
1965	72.86		73.97	55.08		66.17	52.93	
1966	72.16		72.27	54.86		66.12	54.50	
1967	71.98		69.65	53.23		66.28	53.44	
1968	72.29	74.67	65.90	50.91		66.21	52.52	53.36
1969	72.73	74.96		50.58		66.20	51.33	51.80
1970	75.37	78.54		49.60		66.54	48.66	49.07
1971	76.04	77.87		50.00		68.04	47.30	47.91
1972		77.88		49.47		67.67	48.18	48.98
1973		77.18		50.95		67.42		46.55
1974		77.49		53.34		68.16		

Source: For total government expenditures, Table B-1; for central government expenditures, see Table A-2. In OECD terminology, the word "general" is used instead of "total."

Table B-6

FEDERAL GOVERNMENT EXPENDITURES AS A PERCENTAGE OF TOTAL GOVERNMENT EXPENDITURES: DEPARTMENT OF COMMERCE DATA FOR THE UNITED STATES, 1929–1976

1929	25.58	1955	69.56
		1956	68.85
1930	24.97	1957	69.09
1931	33.82	1958	69.70
1932	29.93	1959	69.44
1933	37.21		
1934	49.72	1960	68.26
		1961	68.39
1935	48.85	1962	68.81
1936	53.86	1963	68.04
1937	49.20	1964	67.04
1938	51.29		
1939	50.86	1965	65.92
		1966	67.25
1940	54.08	1967	67.52
1941	71.24	1968	67.15
1942	87.63	1969	65.97
1943	92.02		
1944	92.71	1970	65.46
		1971	64.79
1945	91.21	1972	65.99
1946	78.05	1973	65.45
1947	70.17	1974	65.32
1948	69.13		
1949	69.72	1975	67.09
		1976	67.59
1950	66.94		
1951	72.97		
1952	75.68		
1953	75.93		
1954	71.92		

Source: See source to Table B-4.

Appendix C
TECHNICAL NOTES

1. Discontinuities in Composite Series

As noted in the text of Appendix B, many of the series used in this study (given in Appendix Table B-1) are composites consisting of segments that are based on differing accounting concepts and methods and that have been linked together at some point in time. We discuss here the order of magnitude of discontinuities introduced by this procedure into measures of the fraction of national income attributable to government spending (given in Appendix Table B-3).

One measure of discontinuity is provided by comparing how the percentage of national income attributable to government spending differs between two alternative series in overlapping years, one series being a part of a segment of a composite series and the other being a part of the preceding segment that was discarded in constructing the composite series. Such a comparison is shown in Appendix Table C-1, which is perhaps best explained by a concrete example.

Consider the case of Austria (line 1 of Appendix Table C-1). For 1960–1968, OECD has published two different series of national accounts for Austria, both based on former SNA (as described in Appendix A), the original series (which we call series 1) appearing in yearbooks before 1973 and a revised series (which we call series 2) appearing in yearbooks for 1973 onward. For these years of overlap, the composite series used in this study (as given in Appendix Table B-1) includes series 2, not series 1 (as given in Appendix Table B-2). The percentages of national income attributable to government spending differ as follows when calculated from series 1 and series 2:

	Series 1	Series 2	Difference (series 2 minus series 1)
1960	39.71	39.40	−0.31
1961	40.83	40.25	−0.58
1962	43.41	42.22	−1.19
1963	44.90	43.73	−1.17
1964	46.60	44.73	−1.87
1965	45.78	44.49	−1.29
1966	46.42	45.48	−0.94
1967	48.98	47.97	−1.01
1968	51.30	49.12	−2.18
Sum			−10.54
Average			−1.17

We see that use of series 2 causes the percentage of national income attributable to government spending to be lower in an average year in 1960–1968 by 1.17 percentage points than it would have been if series 1 had been used. We do not consider this difference to be significant relative to the size of government shown by either series.

In general, the average differences do not seem to be significant except for Luxembourg and Switzerland (see Appendix Table C-1). In the case of Luxembourg, we avoided introducing a marked discontinuity by using only the series based on former SNA, instead of constructing a composite series. We could do so since the series based on former SNA runs through 1972. It was not possible to resolve the problem in the same way for Switzerland, since series 1 ends in 1969. It is therefore important in assessing growth of government in Switzerland to keep in mind that the percentage of national income attributable to government spending is recorded in the composite series used in this study as falling more than 4 percentage points in 1968 merely as the result of shifting from one set of national accounts to another.

2. Continuity and Trend in Growth of Government

In Appendix Table C-2, we provide some evidence on how persistently government has grown in our sample of OECD countries. The so-called growth continuity index given there indicates the fraction of years within the period under study in which the size of government— measured by the percentage of national income attributable to total government spending or to domestic government spending—showed an increase over the preceding year. In general, the growth continuity

Table C-1

AVERAGE DIFFERENCE BETWEEN ALTERNATIVE MEASURES OF GOVERNMENT EXPENDITURES AS A PERCENTAGE OF NATIONAL INCOME CALCULATED FROM OVERLAPPING SERIES OF NATIONAL ACCOUNTS: OECD COUNTRIES

	Overlapping Series	Period of Overlap	Average Difference[a] (percentage points)
Austria	Series 1 and 2, former SNA	1960–1968	−1.17
Canada	Former and present SNA	1960–1968	−1.64
Denmark	Former and present SNA	1962–1971	−0.24
France	Series 1 and 2, former SNA	1960–1969	0.12
France	Series 2, former and present SNA	1970–1972	1.95
Federal Republic of Germany	Series 1 and 2, former SNA	1960–1968	−0.59
Luxembourg	Former and present SNA	1968–1972	6.12
Netherlands	Former and present SNA	1968–1969	−1.54
Norway	Former and present SNA	1968–1971	−1.17
Switzerland	Series 1 and 2, former SNA	1968–1969	−4.36
United Kingdom	Former and present SNA	1960–1969	0.47
United States	Former and present SNA	1968–1972	0.15

[a] Sum of annual differences in the period of overlap between the two alternative measures, divided by the number of years in the period of overlap. Each annual difference is the measure in a series in Table B-3 minus the measure derived from a series in Table B-2.

Source: Derived from Tables B-2 and B-3.

Table C-2

CONTINUITY OF GROWTH OF TOTAL GOVERNMENT AND OF DOMESTIC GOVERNMENT EXPENDITURES AS A PERCENTAGE OF NATIONAL INCOME: OECD COUNTRIES

| | Period Covered | Growth Continuity Index[a] | |
		Total government expenditures	Domestic government expenditures
Australia	1960–1974	.57	.57
Austria	1950–1973	.74	.78
Belgium	1953–1974	.67	.76
Canada	1950–1974	.75	.75
Denmark	1950–1974	.75	.71
France	1950–1974	.62	.83
Federal Republic of Germany	1950–1974	.67	.67
Italy	1951–1973	.73	.77
Japan	1952–1974	.64	.64
Luxembourg	1952–1972	.65	.70
Netherlands	1950–1974	.71	.75
Norway	1951–1974	.74	.83
Sweden	1960–1974	.86	.86
Switzerland	1950–1974	.58	. . .
United Kingdom	1950–1974	.58	.71
United States	1950–1973	.57	.65

[a] Ratio of the number of years in which the designated government expenditures rose as a percentage of national income to the total number of years in the period covered.
Ellipsis (. . .): not available.
Source: Derived from Table B-3.

index is higher for growth related to domestic government spending than for growth related to total spending. For the latter case, the index varies from .57 for Australia and the United States to .86 for Sweden. That is to say, in the first case size of government increased in 57 percent of the years over which growth is measured, while in the second case it increased in 86 percent of the years. The median indexes are .67 for total government spending and .75 for domestic government spending.

The results of linear regressions of government expenditures as a percentage of national income on a time trend are summarized in Appendix Tables C-3 and C-4. All regression coefficients are positive

Table C-3

TRENDS IN GOVERNMENT EXPENDITURES AS A PERCENTAGE OF NATIONAL INCOME: LINEAR REGRESSION STATISTICS FOR SIXTEEN OECD COUNTRIES, VARYING PERIODS, 1950–1974

	Constant Term a	Regression Coefficient b	Summary Statistics		Period
			t_b	R^2	
Australia, present SNA	28.9	.46	5.58	.71	1960–1974
Austria					
Composite series	33.4	.66	10.24	.82	1950–1973
Series 1	31.5	.94	15.40	.93	1950–1968
Series 2	40.1	.75	9.12	.87	1960–1973
Belgium, former SNA	27.9	1.00	20.80	.96	1953–1974
Canada					
Composite series	29.8	.82	18.69	.94	1950–1974
Former SNA	30.0	.86	13.81	.92	1950–1968
Present SNA	37.2	.90	9.13	.87	1960–1974
Denmark					
Composite series	19.5	1.42	17.32	.93	1950–1974
Former SNA	20.4	1.33	14.29	.91	1950–1971
Present SNA	31.0	2.18	16.19	.96	1962–1974
France					
Composite series	40.2	.44	11.96	.86	1950–1974
Series 1	39.7	.48	8.25	.79	1950–1974
Series 2	45.1	.31	3.72	.56	1960–1972
Federal Republic of Germany					
Composite series	37.0	.54	12.18	.87	1950–1974
Series 1	37.2	.54	8.12	.79	1950–1968
Series 2	40.7	.73	8.76	.86	1960–1974
Italy, former SNA	29.6	.72	14.66	.91	1951–1973
Japan, former SNA	16.4	.49	10.62	.84	1952–1974
Luxembourg, former SNA	30.9	.92	8.32	.78	1952–1972
Netherlands					
Composite series	31.2	1.13	25.74	.97	1950–1974
Former SNA	31.5	1.10	17.17	.94	1950–1969
Present SNA	50.1	1.56	8.62	.94	1968–1974

Table C-3 (continued)

	Constant Term	Regression Coefficient	Summary Statistics		Period
	a	b	t_b	R^2	
Norway					
Composite series	28.5	1.38	23.81	.96	1951–1974
Former SNA	28.9	1.33	19.87	.95	1951–1971
Present SNA	49.8	2.16	6.40	.89	1968–1974
Sweden, present SNA	35.4	1.84	28.93	.98	1960–1974
Switzerland					
Composite series	20.7	.41	8.39	.74	1950–1974
Series 1	19.2	.62	11.40	.88	1950–1969
Series 2	25.8	.70	4.11	.73	1968–1974
United Kingdom					
Composite series	36.6	.55	5.98	.61	1950–1974
Former SNA	38.0	.37	2.61	.27	1950–1969
Present SNA	38.9	.93	11.25	.91	1960–1974
United States					
Composite series	29.1	.51	9.52	.80	1950–1973
Former SNA	29.0	.52	9.03	.80	1950–1972
Present SNA	39.5	.34	1.10	.23	1968–1973

Note: The form of regression is $GEP = a + b\,T$, where GEP is government expenditures as a percentage of national income, a is the constant term, b is the linear regression coefficient, and T is time in years. The t-statistic for b is signified by t_b and the coefficient of determination by R^2. All t_b are significant at the 95 percent confidence level in a two-tailed test, except the one for the United States, present SNA.

Source: Table B-1 for composite series and designated series for Australia, Belgium, Italy, Japan, Luxembourg, and Sweden; Table B-2 for all other series.

and (except for the one derived from the OECD series for the U.S. based on present SNA and covering 1968–1973) are clearly significant. There seems to be no doubt that the size of government has been trending upward in all sixteen OECD countries studied.

3. Relation between Size and Growth of Government

In Appendix Table C-5, the thirteen OECD countries in our fixed sample are ranked according to size of government in 1953 and growth of government over 1953–1973. There seems to be a marginally significant inverse relation between size of government in

Table C-4

TRENDS IN GOVERNMENT EXPENDITURES AS A PERCENTAGE
OF NATIONAL INCOME: LINEAR REGRESSION STATISTICS
FOR THE UNITED STATES BASED ON DEPARTMENT OF
COMMERCE DATA, VARYING PERIODS, 1929–1975

	Constant Term a	Regression Coefficient b	Summary Statistics	
			t_b	R^2
Total government expenditures: 1929–1975 (excl. 1941–1946)	18.8	.55	15.63*	.86
1929–1940	17.7	.73	2.21*	.26
1947–1975	25.6	.54	11.6*	.83
1960–1975	32.2	.56	7.2*	.77
External government expenditures: 1929–1975 (excl. 1941–1946)	2.9	.24	4.6*	.34
1929–1940	.86	.10	3.9*	.56
1947–1975	12.2	−.11	−1.76	.07
1960–1975	12.2	−.30	−6.46*	.73
Domestic government expenditures: 1929–1975 (excl. 1941–1946)	15.9	.31	5.93*	.46
1929–1940	16.8	.63	1.91	.19
1947–1975	13.5	.65	16.67*	.91
1960–1975	20.1	.85	11.56*	.90

Note: The form of regression is $GEP = a + b\,T$, where GEP is government expenditures as a percentage of national income, a is the constant term, b is the linear regression, and T is time in years. The t-statistic for b is signified by t_b and the adjusted coefficient of determination by R^2. An asterisk (*) denotes that t_b is significant at the 95 percent confidence level in a two-tailed test.

Source: Derived from Table B-4.

Table C-5

RELATION BETWEEN SIZE OF GOVERNMENT IN 1953 AND
GROWTH OF GOVERNMENT OVER 1953–1973:
FIXED SAMPLE OF OECD COUNTRIES

	Rank[a] According to		
	Size of government in 1953[b]	Growth of government in 1953–1973	
		Absolute[c]	Relative[d]
France	1	13	13
United Kingdom	2	11	12
Federal Republic of Germany	3	8	10
Austria	4	7	9
Netherlands	5	3	3
Norway	6	2	2
Canada	7	6	7
United States	8	12	11
Italy	9	4	4
Belgium	10	5	5
Denmark	11	1	1
Switzerland	12	9	8
Japan	13	10	6

[a] In descending order, so that the rank 1 represents the largest magnitude and the rank 13 the smallest.
[b] Measured by the percentage of national income attributable to government spending in 1953.
[c] Increase in size of government between 1953 and 1973.
[d] Absolute growth divided by size of government in 1953.
Source: Derived from Table B-3.

1953 and relative growth of government thereafter, but not between size of government and absolute growth. In the former case, the rank correlation coefficient is -0.544, which is significant at the 94 percent confidence level in a two-tailed test; in the latter case, the coefficient is -0.275, which is significant only at the 65 percent level.

4. Size of Central Government

We present in Appendix Table C-7 the available evidence on trends in centralization of government spending in OECD countries. For many countries, the periods covered by OECD data on central government expenditures are fragmentary, and there are no data at all for

Table C-6

COMPARISON OF DEPARTMENT OF COMMERCE AND OECD SERIES ON CENTRAL[a] GOVERNMENT EXPENDITURES FOR THE UNITED STATES, 1950–1972

(million dollars)

Year	Department of Commerce Series (1)	OECD Series Former SNA (2)	Difference (col. 1 minus col. 2) (3)	Ratio (col. 1 to col. 2) (4)
1950	40,827	36,058	4,769	1.13
1951	57,769	55,048	2,721	1.05
1952	71,052	68,050	3,002	1.04
1953	77,108	73,199	3,909	1.05
1954	69,772	63,851	5,921	1.09
1955	68,142	61,605	6,537	1.11
1956	71,918	64,586	7,332	1.11
1957	79,624	70,390	9,234	1.13
1958	88,933	76,562	12,371	1.16
1959	90,964	78,000	12,964	1.17
1960	93,106	78,527	14,579	1.19
1961	101,944	84,603	17,341	1.20
1962	110,434	92,372	18,062	1.20
1963	114,159	94,778	19,381	1.20
1964	118,182	100,020	18,162	1.18
1965	123,807	102,619	21,188	1.21
1966	143,632	119,245	24,387	1.20
1967	163,676	134,604	29,072	1.22
1968	180,563	147,007	33,556	1.23
1969	188,443	153,200	35,243	1.23
1970	204,194	162,633	41,561	1.26
1971	220,607	171,796	48,811	1.28
1972	244,734	189,990	54,744	1.29

[a] Designated as federal in the Department of Commerce data and central in the OECD data.

Source: For col. 1, see source to Table B-4; for col. 2, see Table A-2.

Belgium and Switzerland. It is also not clear how spending by the central government is defined, as we see from Appendix Table C-6, where data for the United States on central[1] government expenditures from Department of Commerce accounts are compared with those from OECD accounts. The former are consistently larger than the

[1] Designated as federal in the Department of Commerce data and central in the OECD data.

Table C-7

TRENDS IN CENTRAL GOVERNMENT EXPENDITURES AS A
PERCENTAGE OF TOTAL GOVERNMENT EXPENDITURES:
LINEAR REGRESSION STATISTICS FOR FOURTEEN OECD
COUNTRIES, VARYING PERIODS, 1950–1974

	Constant Term a	Regression Coefficient b	Summary Statistics		Period
			t_b	R^2	
Australia, present SNA	67.3	.003	.52	.02	1960–1974
Austria					
Series 1	54.0	−.01	−1.58	.13	1950–1968
Series 2	52.5	−.28	−5.58*	.76	1962–1973
Canada					
Former SNA	65.1	−.64	−7.36*	.76	1950–1968
Present SNA	61.9	−1.58	−2.41*	.31	1960–1974
Denmark, former SNA	59.7	−.001	−.11	.001	1958–1969
France, series 2					
Former SNA	57.6	−.53	−7.00*	.82	1960–1972
Present SNA	57.5	−.15	−.44	.06	1970–1974
Federal Republic of Germany, series 1	43.6	−.52	−4.44*	.54	1950–1968
Italy, former SNA	60.6	−.37	−4.71*	.51	1951–1973
Japan, former SNA	42.3	.36	2.09*	.35	1958–1967
Luxembourg					
Former SNA	67.3	−1.06	−7.41*	.74	1952–1972
Present SNA	51.9	−.36	−1.73	.43	1968–1973
Netherlands, former SNA	31.4	−2.05	−8.12*	.93	1963–1969
Norway					
Former SNA	69.7	.20	5.20*	.59	1951–1971
Present SNA	75.2				
Sweden					
Former SNA	76.9	−.55	−3.54*	.53	1956–1968
Present SNA	58.0	−.58	−5.99*	.73	1960–1974
United Kingdom					
Former SNA	77.9	−.55	−7.51*	.88	1950–1959
Present SNA	70.3	−.28	−2.59*	.34	1960–1974

Table C-7 (continued)

	Constant Term	Regression Coefficient	Summary Statistics		Period
	a	b	t_b	R^2	
United States					
Former SNA	66.0	−.79	−8.20*	.76	1950–1972
Present SNA	54.0	−1.25	−4.89*	.86	1968–1973

Note: The form of regression is $CGP = a + b\,T$, where CGP is central government expenditures as a percentage of total government expenditures, a is the constant term, b is the linear regression coefficient, and T is time in years. The t-statistic for b is signified by t_b and the coefficient of determination by R^2. An asterisk (*) denotes that t_b is significant at the 95 percent confidence level in a two-tailed test.
Source: Derived from Table B-5.

latter, and the difference between the two has grown relatively larger over time. The Commerce data as we have used them count federal grants-in-aid as federal expenditures,[2] whereas the OECD data may not do so, but that possible omission would explain only part of the difference between Commerce and OECD data. In 1972, for example, federal grants-in-aid amounted to $37.5 billion, while the Commerce figure on federal government expenditures exceeds the OECD figure by $54.7 billion. It would seem that the OECD data leave something to be desired in the way of completeness and lack of ambiguity.

The statistics in Appendix Table C-7 summarize the results of fitting linear trends to available series, covering differing time periods, on central government expenditures as a percentage of total government expenditures. It is interesting to note that the trend is downward—the regression coefficient is negative—in eighteen out of twenty-one series, and that the downward trend is statistically significant on the basis of the customary test in fifteen of the eighteen series, those fifteen series applying to eleven countries. The upward trend is shown as significant in two of the three series, those two series applying to Japan and Norway. Despite the shortcomings of the underlying data, it seems reasonable to conclude that, in OECD countries in general, central government expenditures have not accounted for a growing share of total government expenditures since 1950.

---

[2] The grants-in-aid are receipts of state and local governments used to finance commensurate expenditures, but the latter are of course netted out in calculating total government expenditures.

Table C-8

TRENDS IN FEDERAL GOVERNMENT EXPENDITURES AS A
PERCENTAGE OF TOTAL GOVERNMENT EXPENDITURES:
LINEAR REGRESSION STATISTICS FOR THE UNITED STATES,
1929–1975

Period	Constant Term a	Regression Coefficient b	Summary Statistics	
			t_b	R^2
1929–1975 (excl.1941–1946)	44.6	.78	5.88	.47
1929–1940	23.9	2.85	6.90	.82
1947–1975	72.1	−.24	−5.38	.50
1960–1975	68.4	−.19	−4.00	.50

Note: The form of regression is $FGP = a + b\,T$, where FGP is federal government expenditures as a percentage of total government expenditures, a is the constant term, b is the linear regression coefficient, and T is time in years. The t-statistic for b is signified by t_b and the adjusted coefficient of determination by R^2. All t_b are significant at the 95 percent confidence level in a two-tailed test.

Source: Derived from Table B-6.

It would be incautious to leap to the stronger conclusion that faster growth in government spending has been generated at local levels of government than at the central level, because local spending may be encouraged or mandated from the center. In the case of the United States, for example, it has been estimated that each dollar spent in federal grants-in-aid stimulates an additional twenty cents in spending at state and local levels.[3] How much state and local spending is mandated by federal laws and regulations is open to conjecture.

If we use the Department of Commerce data, we also find a downward trend since World War II in federal expenditures as a percentage of total government expenditures in the United States, but it is lower in absolute terms than the trend shown by OECD data (compare Appendix Tables C-7 and C-8). For the entire period 1929–1975, the trend has been markedly upward, of course, the increase from 1929 through 1940 far exceeding the decline since 1947.

[3] See James M. Buchanan and Richard E. Wagner, *Democracy in Deficit* (New York: Academic Press, 1977), p. 77, n. 2.

Cover and book design: Pat Taylor